Word in Season

Scripture Memory Tools

Devotional Bible Studies by
Penelope J. Stokes

World Wide Publications
A ministry of the Billy Graham Evangelistic Association
1303 Hennepin Ave., Minneapolis, Minnesota 55403

Words in Season

World Wide Publications is the publishing ministry of the Billy Graham Evangelistic Association.

Scripture quotations marked KJV are from the King James version of the Bible.

Scripture quotations not marked, or marked NIV, are taken from The Holy Bible, New International Version, copyright © 1973, 1978, 1984, International Bible Society. Used by permission of Zondervan Bible Publishers.

ISBN 0-89066-139-1

Printed in the United States of America

Contents

Why Memorize?

Many people believe that they "simply can't memorize Scripture." They seem to have a mental block that prevents them from committing the Word of God to memory.

Memorization does not have to be a drudgery, an unwelcome task that just "has to be done" if we are to be spiritually mature. In fact, no spiritual discipline is a "requirement" for God's favor. But memorizing Scripture can be a tremendous asset to a Christian's life. When we know the Word of God and apply it, we can experience radical change in our lives.

People often try (with little success) to learn Scripture "in a vacuum." They choose isolated Scriptures and try to memorize them without thinking of the context or application of those verses. Although they may remember the verses for a time, they often fail to retain them for long, because the verses have no practical meaning for them.

This study is an attempt to put Scripture memory in perspective—to combine it with Bible study and application so that the verses are not taken out of context or chosen simply as "favorites." Each day, a verse or two is presented in light of a brief Bible teaching, along with questions to stimulate insight and application. (If Scripture memorization is a completely new endeavor for you, perhaps you'll want to try just two or three verses a week at first.) The study is designed to be used alone, but it can easily be adapted for small groups.

The verses and studies in this book are designed to help you grow in your commitment to Jesus Christ, and to know him better. May the Lord extend his grace and light to you as you seek to go deeper in his Word.

Keys for Memorizing Scripture

. Identify the subject. Look carefully at the context of the verse. Make sure you understand what the writer is saying.

. Repeat the verse. Memorization is accomplished through repetition. The more you review the verse, the more clearly it will be impressed upon your mind.

. Subdivide the verse. Break the verse down into its component parts. Repeat each part again and again, thinking carefully about its meaning. Then join that part to the next part of the verse.

. Visualize the circumstances. Try to get a mental picture of the circumstances of the verse: Jesus speaking to his disciples, Paul writing from a dark jail, Isaiah prophesying on a mountaintop. Put the verse into that picture—what did it mean for those who heard it first?

. Keep the Word in front of you. Tear off each day's verse card (from the middle section of this book) and tape it to your shaving mirror, your dashboard, your typewriter. Say the verses as you drive, wash dishes, walk in your neighborhood. The Scriptures become more real as we build them into our daily lives.

. Review the verses aloud. Speaking the Word of God aloud has an amazing power of persuasion. Try emphasizing different words in the verse; each verse carries various shades of meaning with differing emphasis.

. Apply the verses to your life. The questions at the end of each study should help you apply each of the verses. Share your insights with others; keep a "spiritual growth journal" that traces the changes in your life. As you use the verses you learn, they become part of you—not just a memory exercise, but living truth that makes a difference in your life.

. Review. A brief review checklist is provided at the end of each week to help you remember the significance of that week's verses. Use the checklist to remind yourself of the truth of God's Word, and to keep the verses you have memorized fresh in your mind.

Day 1—God's Perspective

Memory Verse: Philippians 4:13
I can do everything through him who gives me strength.

Many of us live out self-fulfilling prophecies. We believe what we tell ourselves—or what we have been told by others: "You're stupid," "You're ugly," "You'll never amount to anything," "You can't do anything right."
We program ourselves for spiritual failure as well. "I just can't memorize Scripture," we say. "It comes and goes, and I can't seem to get it to stay." Yet daily we memorize volumes of information that is less significant than the Scriptures—telephone numbers, identification codes, song lyrics, advertising jingles.

     The answer to the dilemma of negativism is not *positive* thinking, but *right* thinking— biblical thinking, according to what the Bible reveals of God's perspective. God says, "You are worthwhile. You are valued. You are loved. I created you just as you are, and whatever I call you to do, I will give you the strength to do it."

     The context of Philippians 4:13 shows that Paul had learned this important secret of spiritual strength. Paul had known poverty and plenty, trouble and victory. But he also knew he did not have to let circumstances determine his response to God's will. Rather than believing the messages he received through difficulty, rejection, even imprisonment, Paul believed the Word of God. His circumstances may have looked bad, but he knew that God was good.

     We need not be controlled by the negative messages life throws into our paths—even those self-defeating pronouncements we make to ourselves.   Rather, we can respond according to God's perspective, with the conviction that God has given us the strength we need to meet the challenges we face.

Application

1. What challenges do I face that make me realize my own insufficiencies? Is memorizing Scripture one of those challenges for me?

2. How does today's memory verse help me face those challenges?

Day 2—Growing Up

Memory Verses: 2 Timothy 3:16-17
All Scripture is God-breathed and is useful for teaching, rebuking, correcting and training in righteousness, so that the man of God may be thoroughly equipped for every good work.

"I can't wait till I get big!" Marc, age five, declared. "Then I can do what I want!" Most of us, as children, shared Marc's sentiment. We looked forward to that "magic age"—sixteen, eighteen, twenty-one—when we would be adults: mature, able to make our own decisions.

We find, of course, that adulthood has its own share of difficulties and conflict. But even in our spiritual lives we often long for a "magic moment" of maturity. As one woman confessed, "Ever since I became a Christian, I've hoped I'd wake up one morning to find myself *mature.*"

But growth in the spiritual life comes gradually, like growth in the physical world. In 2 Timothy 3:16-17, Paul gives the young pastor Timothy an important key to spiritual growing up—the Word of God.

The Word is "profitable" or "useful," Paul says, for "teaching"—that is, for developing a right concept of God. Scripture offers "rebuke" when we go wrong, "correction" to set us on the right path, and "training in righteousness" so that we can grow in the image of Christ.

The purpose of Scripture's work in our lives, Paul emphasizes, is that we may be "perfect"—mature, equipped for the good things God has for us to do. Such maturity does not come easily or instantaneously, but it does come—sometimes imperceptibly—as we submit our lives to the transforming power of God's Word.

Application

1. In what areas of my life do I need to grow? How can I benefit from the Bible's
   a. teaching?
   b. rebuke?
   c. correction?
   d. training in righteousness?

2. How can memorizing God's Word help me grow in those areas?

Day 3—Let the Word Dwell in You

Memory Verse: Colossians 3:16
Let the word of Christ dwell in you richly as you teach and admonish one another with all wisdom, and as you sing psalms, hymns and spiritual songs with gratitude in your hearts to God.

Every day, whether we are aware of it or not, our minds are bombarded by twentieth-century values: "Dress for success!" "Get ahead!" "You deserve a break today. . . ." Television, radio, and the incessant voices that surround us distract our attention and keep us from focusing on what is really important in our lives.

Paul's instruction to the Colossian church brings us back to God's value system: "Let the word of Christ dwell in you richly."

When we give attention to the Word of God, we put ourselves in a position to hear a higher truth than the clamor of immediate demands and the expectations of the world around us. We can experience peace in the midst of struggle and rest in a restless environment. God's Word is a powerful force for good in our lives—not merely an attractive philosophy, but true power to overcome the pressures of daily life.

Dwelling on the Word of God, and letting it indwell us, takes many forms. Scripture memory, music, meditation, talking with others about the goodness of God all help us keep our attention focused on Christ rather than on the values of the world around us.

We can choose to listen to Christian radio or tapes. We can take time daily for quiet meditation on his Word. We can commit the Word to memory and draw on its power during the day. And as we listen to the voice of the Spirit rather than the noise around us, we can enter into his peace and live in communion with him.

Application

1. What pressures do I face that tend to distract me from the reality of Christ's presence?

2. How can I "let the word of Christ dwell richly" in me, so that I can regain my focus on him?

3. What practical changes can I make in my life to help me focus my attention on Jesus and his Word?

Day 4—Arming for Battle

Memory Verse: Joshua 1:8
Do not let this Book of the Law depart from your mouth; meditate on it day and night, so that you may be careful to do everything written in it. Then you will be prosperous and successful.

When God spoke these words to Joshua, the young leader's prospects for "prosperity" and "success" were far from promising. Upon Moses' death, Joshua was appointed to lead Israel into the Promised Land, to claim the territory and establish a nation under God's rule.

Joshua was afraid, and for good reason. The people were rebellious and intractable. And "claiming the land" meant battling many strong enemies. Yet God told Joshua that his strength would come not in preparing for battle, but in preparing himself by meditating on and applying God's Word to his life.

We, too, face difficult battles as we seek to enter the "Promised Land" of God's peace and presence. But his promise is the same as it was to Joshua: through obedience to the Word, we can find prosperity and success.

God's promise does not necessarily mean financial prosperity or material success. Those victories may come as well, but God's primary purpose for his people is spiritual success—the victory and joy of living in fellowship with him. We can be enriched in the knowledge of God and find power to overcome the enemies of sin and self. The way may not be easy—after all, there is no victory without a conflict—but God promises that we will succeed as we look to him.

Application

1. What image do I have of a personal "Promised Land" that I long to enter and claim as my own?

2. What enemies will I need to battle in order to enter that land?

3. How can meditation on the Word of God and obedience to him bring me prosperity and success?

Day 5—Learning by Heart

Memory Verses: Psalm 119:9,11
How can a young man keep his way pure? By living according to your word. I have hidden your word in my heart that I might not sin against you.

"His heart is just not in it," a gifted musician commented about the pianist onstage. "He's here at Orchestra Hall, playing for thousands of people, and his technique is flawless, but something is missing—his heart just isn't in it."

The psalmist, in Psalm 119, draws a similar parallel. We can "keep our way pure" through obedience to the Word, by ordering our lives according to the commands of the Scripture. But outward behavior is not the only essential factor in purity of life. The changes in our behavior need to come from the *heart,* from the inside out. Our "technique" for living the Christian life may be flawless, but unless our obedience is founded in heart motivation, something is certainly missing.

"I seek you with all my heart," the psalmist declares in verse 10. Thus he can say in verse 11, "I have hidden your word in my heart that I might not sin against you."

Often we refer to memorization as "learning by heart"—and indeed, "by heart" is the biblical mandate for assimilating God's truth into our daily lives. "By rote" or "by mind" leaves us intellectually overstuffed, yet spiritually starving.

When we try to apply the Word outwardly to our behavior, we end up in a tangle of legalism, a long "do list" by which we hope to please God. But when we set our *hearts* toward God first, then changes in our behavior grow out of love for God and a deep desire to serve him. Then we are truly loving and obeying God with our whole hearts.

Application

1. In what ways have I tried to apply God's Word to my *behavior* without having the truth firmly in my *heart*? What was the result?

2. How can I set my heart toward God and give myself more fully to his Word?

3. What areas of my life need "purifying"? How can these verses help me to "make my way pure"?

Day 6—Shielded by the Word

Memory Verse: Proverbs 30:5
Every word of God is flawless; he is a shield to those who take refuge in him.

A wife of ten years, betrayed by her husband's infidelity, declares that she will never trust a man again. A teenage son says of his father, "I just can't depend on him anymore! Dad always talks big and makes promises, but he never does what he says." A career woman, her reputation undermined by gossip, leaves the church broken, and never returns.

Human beings are weak, volatile, unfaithful creatures; often we break our word and hurt others in the process. But the Scripture clearly assures us that God's Word is not like the word of man. God always remains faithful to his Word, always fulfills his promises, always does what he says he will do.

God's Word is pure or "flawless," Proverbs 30:5 says. His Word is not distorted with mixed motives or flawed by untruth. God's Word is dependable, able to support and lift us up, able to speak encouragement to us. His Word is a "shield" a protection for us against the onslaughts of the Enemy, a place of refuge from the struggle and confusion of daily life.

We live in a world that recognizes no absolute truth. Morality, values, relationships, ethics—every decision of life, it seems, "depends upon the situation." But in the midst of the confusion, God interjects his Word—timeless, pure, trustworthy, reliable.

We can depend upon God's Word. We can turn to him to verify who we are and the purposes for which we were created. We can find refuge in his truth, and rest in the knowledge that whatever he says, he will do.

Application

1. In my own experience, how have I found God's Word to be different from the word of men and women?

2. In what areas of my life do I need the assurance of the validity and dependability of God's Word?

3. How can today's verse help me trust more fully in God's Word?

Day 7—The Cost of Wisdom

Memory Verses: Proverbs 4:4,7

He taught me and said, "Lay hold of my words with all your heart; keep my commands and you will live. Wisdom is supreme; therefore get wisdom. Though it cost all you have, get understanding."

Establishing priorities is a popular topic of conversation in our generation. We carry appointment calendars and attend goal-setting strategy seminars. We let machines answer our telephones so that we won't miss any important messages, or so that we can screen calls before we answer them. We order our lives so that we can "get ahead."

"Getting ahead" in God's kingdom, however, involves other priorities than the ones we may set for ourselves. "Wisdom is supreme," the principal thing, says Proverbs 4:7. "Get wisdom. Though it cost all you have, get understanding."

Wisdom is defined as "an understanding of what is true, right, or lasting." Biblical wisdom is not merely the accumulation of facts about God and his teaching, but the application of those truths to life, taking on the character of God as we mature in the image of Christ.

Such wisdom may, indeed, come at great cost. Jesus calls us to "lay down our lives" to follow him—perhaps not literally to die, but to die to self-centered priorities, to allow the Holy Spirit to establish his value system in us.

"Keep my commandments and you will live," verse 4 of Proverbs 4 says. Real life—rich, fulfilling, significant, abundant life—comes only through union with God. The success offered by the world, the acclaim of others, material prosperity and convenience cannot satisfy us once we have tasted the joy of life with God in Christ.

Application

1. What does "getting wisdom" mean to me?

2. What practical changes can I make in my life to help me focus my attention on the priorities and values of the Lord?

Reviewing This Week

Verses   **Personal Application**

Philippians 4:13

2 Timothy 3:16-17

Colossians 3:16

Joshua 1:8

Psalm 119:9,11

Proverbs 30:5

Proverbs 4:4,7

Day 1—Sin Universal

Memory Verses: Romans 3:23-24
For all have sinned and fall short of the glory of God, and are justified freely by his grace through the redemption that came by Christ Jesus.

A distinguished middle-aged man stood trembling before his church to give his testimony. Years before, in the grip of a mental illness that nearly destroyed his life, he had taken the life of his own daughter and tried to kill himself. But he did not die; tried and convicted, he spent years in prison, and even longer in the prison of his own guilt. After the service, a young woman walked up to him and said simply, "Thank you for sharing. I've sinned, too."

We've all sinned, too—lest we forget or rationalize, the Bible reminds us in no uncertain terms. And the writer of these verses was no stranger to sin: he was the Pharisee, the holier-than-thou religious leader who officiated at the stoning death of Stephen. He was the Jew who had scattered and killed the followers of this heretic called the Christ. He thought he was righteous while he murdered God's people.

Christians tend to establish a "hierarchy" of sin—sexual sin is "worse" than pride; murder is "more horrible" than slander. Yet the Bible gives no indication that God acknowledges our hierarchy. Sin is sin; all have sinned, and if we are guilty at one point, we are guilty of all.

Rather than rationalize our individual sins as being "less bad" than someone else's, we need to openly confess our dilemma as sinners and turn to God for his remedy. We are, he declares, "justified freely by his grace" (v. 24). We cannot and do not need to earn or deserve that grace—it is a gift from God.

Application

1. Have I ever compared my sin with someone else's in order to make myself feel like a better person? Why is such comparison not a valid remedy for sin?

2. Why do I need to acknowledge my sin honestly before I can receive justification?

3. How can these verses help me keep my own sin in perspective—that is, keep me from comparing myself to others, and help me be honest with God?

Day 2—Earning Death

Memory Verse: Romans 6:23
For the wages of sin is death, but the gift of God is eternal life in Christ Jesus our Lord.

"I only want my rights," declares the belligerent Big Ghost, one of the characters in C. S. Lewis's classic, *The Great Divorce*. "I'm not asking for anybody's bleeding charity."

"Then do. At once," his angelic friend Len urges. "Ask for the Bleeding Charity. Everything is here for the asking and nothing can be bought."[1]

Often we are much like the Ghost in Lewis's tale of heaven and hell. We want "what we deserve," and being blind to our own sin, we think we deserve praise, or at least mercy. But Paul is very clear on what we have coming: "The wages of sin is death."

We work for our wages—we've earned our paycheck, and we deserve it. We don't have to thank anyone for paying us—it's our due, not a gift. Similarly, the paycheck issued to us in remuneration for our sin is what we deserve: death.

Yet, if we are willing to lay aside our pride and accept God's gift, we can live. "The gift of God is eternal life." Nothing we can do or say can make us worthy of the gift of life. We are sinners by nature and we rebel against God in our choices. Yet God, in Christ, offers grace to us, freedom from sin, liberty from the burden of trying to earn his favor.

Ironically, freedom and peace in the Christian life come not through justifying ourselves and making ourselves look good, but through acknowledging the depth of our sin and our inability to do anything about it. When we realize that we are trapped in our sinful selves and only Christ can free us, then we are ready to journey toward grace and freedom.

Application

1. In what ways have I tried to "earn" the gift of eternal life?

2. What can I do to focus on God's grace and realize that I cannot accomplish my own salvation?

[1]C. S. Lewis, *The Great Divorce* (New York: Macmillan, 1946), 34.

Day 3—The Remedy

Memory Verse: Acts 4:12
Salvation is found in no one else, for there is no other name under heaven given to men by which we must be saved.

"You have cancer," the doctor told his patient. "We need to operate—as soon as possible. It's the only remedy." The patient, not wanting to undergo surgery unless it was absolutely necessary, sought out a second opinion, then a third. When the third round of testing came up with the same results, she returned to her doctor and submitted herself to the treatment.

Often the remedy for problems in our lives seems worse than the problems themselves. We don't want to endure the pain of self-examination, of honest confrontation with our sin and selfishness. We'd rather live on in "blissful ignorance" than face up to ourselves.

But the Bible tells us that there is only one remedy for sin: casting ourselves upon the saving grace of God in Jesus Christ. Submitting ourselves to God's "treatment" for sin is not an easy matter or a simple decision. We have to give up on ourselves, on our own striving for self-salvation. We have to come to the agonizing realization of our sin, the depths to which we have fallen.

Acknowledging sin is not a duty simply for "bad" people who have lived in rebellion against God. "Good" people—Sunday-school kids, moral parents, and sweet little grand-mothers—may have more difficulty coming to Christ than swindlers and prostitutes, precisely because their sin is not as visible—sometimes it is even applauded by church and society.

"Good" or "bad," we all have the same problem: sin. And, because of the Lord's grace, we all have the same remedy: salvation through Christ. As we look to him, not to others, and see ourselves in light of his holiness, we can glimpse the seriousness of our own resistance to him and call upon his name.

Application

1. What other "remedies" have I tried to use in treating my sin?

2. Why is Jesus Christ the only source of salvation?

3. How can this verse help me see the "salvation" of Christ in the daily struggles of life?

Day 4—Entire Forgiveness

Memory Verse: Acts 13:38
Therefore, my brothers, I want you to know that through Jesus the forgiveness of sins is proclaimed to you.

At age seventeen Mary, a cross-country runner, was diagnosed with multiple sclerosis. She went on to college, faced with the prospect of gradual physical decline and, ultimately, life in a wheelchair. "The worst part," Mary admitted, "is not the pain or the inability to do what I once did. The worst part is the hopelessness, the emotional struggle. There is no cure, no real treatment—only endurance."

In our fallen world, there are many incurable circumstances we simply have to endure. But the guilt of our sin is not one of them. Yet despite the declaration of Scripture that Jesus' sacrificial death paid the price for our sins, many of us carry around a load of guilt—as if we ourselves had to pay the price.

Paul, a man who knew the grace of God and the depth of his own sin, emphasizes the source and completeness of our forgiveness: "Through Jesus the forgiveness of sins is proclaimed to you."

Through Jesus—not through my good behavior, not through my determination to change, not through my reputation, my family's faith, or my religious duties. Forgiveness of sins comes through Christ alone, a gift which we do not deserve, a gift which places all of us on equal ground at the foot of the cross.

To acknowledge our sin without knowing the source of forgiveness only results in hopelessness and despair—we see ourselves, yet we are powerless to change the sin we see. But when we realize that Christ has provided complete forgiveness for sin, we can face our sin honestly, knowing the freedom of confession and the restoration of forgiveness.

Application

1. In what ways have I tried to change myself, to "turn over a new leaf," to "make myself worthy" of God's love?

2. How can today's memory verse help me remember the source of forgiveness?

Day 5—It Is Finished!

Memory Verse: John 5:24
I tell you the truth, whoever hears my word and believes him who sent me has eternal life and will not be condemned; he has crossed over from death to life.

"PLEASE BE PATIENT—GOD IS NOT FINISHED WITH ME YET," the sweatshirt read. In this case, the message was an ironic one, for the occupant of the shirt was a snaggle-toothed, freckle-faced six year old!

In one sense, God is not finished with the work he has to do in each of us. Life in Christ is an ongoing process of change and growth as we become more like him. Certainly, the more we see of ourselves, the more we *hope* he isn't finished with us!

Yet whatever plans God has for making us into the men and women he created us to be, certain aspects of our life in Christ *are* finished, finalized. Jesus declares with absolute assurance, "Whoever hears my word and believes him who sent me has eternal life and will not be condemned; he has crossed over from death to life."

Because we do not have to earn or deserve God's grace, because we are not called to prove ourselves worthy of salvation, we can have immediate and total assurance of the security of life in Jesus Christ. The one who puts his trust in the Lord *has* eternal life; he *will not be condemned*; he *has crossed over* from death to life.

This "crossing over" into life happens in the split second when we acknowledge our dependence upon Christ alone. And the rest of our lives is given over to the development of his image in us.

God is not finished with us yet. But his work of salvation is finished—complete, fully dependable, an accomplished fact.

Application

1. Have I ever doubted the "accomplished fact" of my own salvation? Why?

2. How can today's verse help me realize that, although I may have a lot of growing yet to do, my salvation in Jesus Christ is secure?

Day 6—Starting Over

Memory Verse: 2 Corinthians 5:17
Therefore, if anyone is in Christ, he is a new creation; the old has gone, the new has come!

"The trouble with turning over a new leaf," Gordon sighed, "is that once you've done it twice, you're right back where you started." Gordon, in his mid-fifties, had his job "canceled" by a company wanting to cut back on retirement payments. Out of work, with few prospects, he said wistfully, "I wish I had the chance to start over again."

Many of us would echo Gordon's sentiments. Whether we have lost a job, gone through a divorce, moved to another part of the country, or experienced some lesser crisis, we often long for the chance to begin again, fresh, without the shadow of past mistakes following us.

God's Word offers just such an opportunity. Anyone who is in Christ, Paul says in 2 Corinthians 5:17, is a "new creation." For the Christian, the past is truly past—"all things are become new." In the forgiveness and restoration of God's grace we can leave the past behind, with all its mistakes, and enter into new life.

And the promise is not just for the newly saved. Those of us who have been Christians for years need to hear the truth of 2 Corinthians 5:17 again, for we have accumulated some "new mistakes" since we came to Christ. *Anyone* who is in Christ is a new creation; the freedom of forgiveness, of "starting over" is available to all who call upon the name of the Lord.

We cannot ever really "start over" simply by establishing New Year's resolutions or turning over a new leaf. Only God gives us that opportunity; his grace allows us to clear away the rubble of the past and begin again. Everything becomes new in God's loving forgiveness.

Application

1. What "resolutions" have I made in an attempt to "start over" in some area of struggle or failure in my life? Did my resolutions work?

2. What does 2 Corinthians 5:17 mean for me at this point in my Christian life?

Day 7—Oh, Freedom!

Memory Verses: Romans 8:1-2
Therefore, there is now no condemnation for those who are in Christ Jesus, because through Christ Jesus the law of the Spirit of life set me free from the law of sin and death.

In the classic movie, *I Want to Live!* actress Susan Hayward plays a woman convicted of murder and sentenced to be executed. The suspense builds; the execution is delayed as the officials wait for word of a pardon. Finally, the woman is executed; the call comes, and the pardon has been granted, but it is too late.

When no pardon is granted, condemnation leads to death. Our sin marks us as "guilty" before God, and we deserve the wages of that sin, which is death. But in Jesus Christ, the pardon does come—and it comes in time. Our sin deserves condemnation by God, and yet he forgives us because Christ paid the penalty for us.

But we face other kinds of condemnation as well—self-condemnation, that internal accusation that we still, somehow, must pay the price for our own sin. Others often condemn us as well, offering much less forgiveness and mercy than God does. And the Enemy of our souls condemns us, trying to convince us that we don't, after all, have real freedom from sin.

Yet Paul tells us in Romans 8, "there is now *no condemnation* for those who are in Christ Jesus" (italics added). God has forgiven us freely; he has granted his pardon. And in light of his forgiveness, how can we live under the condemnation of others—or even of ourselves?

We are free, Paul says—free from the "law of sin and death," free to live in the liberty of the Spirit. The stay of execution has come; the pardon has been granted. Never again can we be tried for the same crimes; never again must we live under the burden of condemnation.

Application

1. Have I ever lived under the burden of condemnation from myself or others? Why?

2. How can Romans 8:1-2 help me live in freedom from such condemnation?

Reviewing This Week

Verses   **Personal Application**

Romans 3:23-24

Romans 6:23

Acts 4:12

Acts 13:38

John 5:24

2 Corinthians 5:17

Romans 8:1-2

Day 1—Bought Back

Memory Verse: Ephesians 1:7
In him we have redemption through his blood, the forgiveness of sins, in accordance with the riches of God's grace.

In the opening scenes of *The Glenn Miller Story,* Glenn Miller, then a struggling musician trying to find an audience for his music, enters a pawn shop. He has hocked his trombone for rent money, and has come to redeem it. Paying the pawn broker the money, he buys back his own instrument and leaves the shop, indicating that he will probably be back again.

In Ephesians 1:7, Paul says that in Christ "we have redemption through his blood, the forgiveness of sins, in accordance with the riches of God's grace." We belonged to God from the beginning; he made us and stamped his image upon us. But through sin we were lost, pawned to the world's system and the Enemy of our souls.

But God redeemed us; he "bought us back" with the most valuable currency in the universe—the blood of his own Son, Jesus Christ. He did not resent the bargain, or question whether we were worth such a price. He freely gave Jesus in trade to ransom the souls of the people he had created and loved.

Sometimes in Christian circles we get so caught up in religious jargon that we forget what redemption really means. God did not *have* to "get us out of hock." He was not compelled to buy us back when we had sold ourselves to sin. But because of his love, and with no deserving on our part, he chose to pay an enormous price to set us free. We are redeemed, bought back, by the One who owned us in the first place.

Application

. In what ways have I been "in hock" to sin in my life?

. What does it mean, in practical terms, that God "redeemed" me from that sin?

Day 2—The Right of Family

Memory Verses: John 1:11-12

He came to that which was his own, but his own did not receive him. Yet to all who received him, to those who believed in his name, he gave the right to become children o *God.*

"Dad, can I ask you something?" Jimmy leaned across the back of his father's chair. His father lowered the newspaper and reached around, settling Jimmy on his lap.

"Sure, Son," he answered. "You can ask me anything you want. The answer might not be *Yes,* but you always have the right to ask."

For many who have grown up in homes where the father was absent, or when present, abusive or silent, the scenario of Jimmy and his father may seem unrealistic. Often we *aren't* given the right by our parents to ask for what we want, to communicate openly, to express our needs and desires.

But God clearly indicates that no matter what our human families have been like, in his family there are no barriers to belonging, to open communication. When we commit our lives to Christ and submit to his lordship, we have the *right* to become the sons and daughters of God.

In Christ, we have the right to approach him, to pray, to seek wisdom, to ask advice, to make requests, to verbalize our needs and desires. We don't have to be afraid of sounding stupid or being rejected, because in Christ we belong to him, and he loves us.

The KJV uses the word "power" in verse 12—"to them gave he *power* to become the sons of God." Power implies ability, that we are equipped by the Spirit to be children of the King. We have the *right* and we have the *power* to become who God has called us to be—his children.

Application

1. Under what circumstances in my life have I felt that I didn't have the right to express my wishes or feelings?

2. How do today's verses give me confidence in approaching God?

Day 3—Inseparable From God's Love

Memory Verses: Romans 8:38-39
For I am convinced that neither death nor life, neither angels nor demons, neither the present nor the future, nor any powers, neither height nor depth, nor anything else in all creation, will be able to separate us from the love of God that is in Christ Jesus our Lord.

Separation is a fact of human life. Relationships disintegrate, children grow up, loved ones die, husbands and wives divorce, friends change and drift apart. We may resist change and separation, but we must deal with them nevertheless.

Separation sometimes is a natural result of growth and development; sometimes it is a violent, cataclysmic shaking of an individual's life. Two lifelong friends go separate ways to college or into future careers; a church splits over doctrinal differences; a wife finds out a hidden secret in her husband's past.

But with God, there is no separation, no death, no breaking of vows, no growing beyond the relationship. Nothing, says Paul, can separate us from the love of God. A skeleton in my closet, once revealed, may cost me the trust of those I thought were my friends. But God knows all my past, all my sin; he forgives, and it cannot separate me from him.

My present personal struggles may cause trouble in my job and result in the loss of that income, but God understands what I'm going through, and even when I'm angry at him, he can take it without drawing away or striking back. My present problems cannot separate me from the Lord.

And God knows, too, the plan he has established for my future. I cannot walk away from him, grow beyond my need for him, or outrun him into tomorrow.

Sin may separate me from my awareness of God's presence in my life, but it cannot set me beyond his reach. There is no power that is greater than God's love, and no place I can go that will separate me from that love.

Application

1. Have I ever felt separated from the love of God? Under what circumstances?

2. How can today's verses free me from anxiety about the past, the present, or the future?

Day 4—Daddy!

Memory Verse: Romans 8:15

For you did not receive a spirit that makes you a slave again to fear, but you received the Spirit of sonship. And by him we cry, "Abba, Father."

"I've always been a Daddy's girl," Sandi said proudly, and her relationship with her father proved it. She was never spoiled, but even as a grown woman, Sandi maintained a closeness with her father, sharing intimately with him the important issues of her life. And just her use of the name "Daddy" indicated that he was, indeed, a warm, approachable, affectionate man.

Many people are not so fortunate. Some fathers are stern and harsh; others absent or uncaring, some even abusive. Few have the kind of father who presents a picture of the loving fatherhood of God.

But whatever our concept of fatherhood, God makes clear that he is everything we always wanted our fathers to be—loving, forgiving, approachable, totally accepting of us as we are, encouraging us to become all he has created us to be.

In Romans 8, Paul calls God our "Abba Father." The Aramaic word for Father, *Abba,* is an intimate term that might well be translated, *Daddy*. God is our "Daddy," our "Abba"—not a distant, stern patriarch ready to strike us down at the first sign of transgression, but a gentle, loving Father who longs for us to climb into his lap and let him comfort us.

When we commit ourselves to Christ, Paul indicates, we do not receive a "spirit of bondage to fear" but a "spirit of adoption." We are not called to respond to God out of fear, but out of love and reverence. We can relax and enjoy his presence, for we are his children, and he is our loving Daddy.

Application

1. What concept of fatherhood do I have from my own experience with my father? How does that correspond to Paul's description of God as "Daddy"?

2. How can this verse help change my perception of what it means to have God as my Father?

Day 5—God Loved, So He Gave

Memory Verses: John 3:16-17

For God so loved the world that he gave his one and only Son, that whoever believes in him shall not perish but have eternal life. For God did not send his Son into the world to condemn the world, but to save the world through him.

Often called "the gospel in a nutshell," John 3:16 is so familiar, even to the unchurched, that it has all but lost its impact for us. We recite it by rote, as if it had no more meaning than a social security number, and think that we understand the truth because we know the words.

Why did God send Jesus, his only Son, into the world to die? Because *he loved the people he had created.* God had no reason, humanly speaking, to love mankind. Throughout history, from the Garden of Eden forward, people had deliberately turned against God and tried his patience. Even the nation God chose for himself, Israel, rebelled against the Lord and turned to other gods.

And we, as individuals, have rebelled against him too. We have tried to control our own lives; we have denied his reality; or acknowledged his existence and then systematically ignored him. We have become our own gods.

Yet Christ, in love, took upon himself the rejection, the humiliation, the pain we were responsible for. We deserved to be condemned to die, but he died for us instead. "God did not send his Son into the world to condemn the world," John 3:17 says, "but to save the world through him."

Often, even after we have committed our lives to Christ, we mistakenly suppose that God's primary purpose is to condemn us—to catch us in sin and punish us. But God says that his purpose is to love us and to save us from sin and from ourselves. He loved, and so he gave; he still loves, and he still continues to give.

Application

1. What sin in my life put Jesus on the cross for me?

2. How do I know that my sin has been forgiven?

3. How can these verses help me when I face condemnation and guilt?

Day 6—Eternal Life, Beginning Now

Memory Verse: John 10:28
I give them eternal life, and they shall never perish; no one can snatch them out of my hand.

In C. S. Lewis's *The Great Divorce,* one of the spirits in heaven, identifying himself as George MacDonald, makes some startling statements on the nature of eternal life. Depending upon the individual's choice for or against Christ, MacDonald says, everything in life takes on the character of heaven or hell. "At the end of all things, when the sun rises here (in heaven) and the twilight turns to blackness down there, the Blessed will say, 'We have never lived anywhere except in Heaven,' and the Lost, 'We were always in Hell.' And both will speak truly."[2]

   Lewis was not trying to make a theological case, but to demonstrate a principle: eternal life begins *now*. The choices that we make for or against obedience to God, the life we live, the patterns we establish, all move us in one direction or the other.

   And when we have decided to choose obedience to God, when we give ourselves fully into his hands, he is able to take the worst of circumstances and redeem them for our good, use them to mature us in his image. "I give them eternal life," Jesus says in John 10:28, "and they shall never perish; no one can snatch them out of my hand."

   In Christ is a very secure place to be. No experience is lost, no pain is wasted. Everything in our lives is redeemed by God for our benefit.

Application

1. How have I experienced the truth that "eternal life begins now"?

2. How can this verse help me put life in perspective during times of stress and anxiety?

[2]C. S. Lewis, *The Great Divorce* (New York: Macmillan, 1946), 68.

Day 7—The Great Exchange

Memory Verse: 2 Corinthians 5:21
God made him who had no sin to be sin for us, so that in him we might become the righteousness of God.

People were talking; the gossip lines were busy day and night. Andrea, a Bible study leader and pillar of the church, had been accused of indiscretion with a married man, another member of the congregation. The rumors were proved untrue, but that hardly mattered anymore. The damage was done.

"It's just not fair," Andrea said. "It was all so unnecessary. And now, even though I've done nothing wrong, my relationship with that church will never be the same again."

We all know what pain is caused by undeserved accusation, rejection, and misunderstanding. Sometimes, when the smoke clears, irreparable damage has been done, even when no sin has occurred. We can understand the torment that comes when we've sinned, but when we've done nothing wrong, the injustice may seem unbearable.

Jesus knew what it was to suffer unjustly. He had never sinned at all, yet he "became sin" for us. He gave himself in an outrageous exchange: he took our sin and gave us his righteousness.

Living in this exchange does not mean, of course, that we will be exempt from pain, that we will never again suffer unjustly or be subject to rejection. But in Christ, we are *declared* righteous before God, just as Jesus himself is righteous. And as we submit to the Holy Spirit's work in us, we *become* righteous, obeying him and growing in grace. Christ endured rejection for us so that we might live in him.

Application

1. Have I ever suffered unjustly or been rejected by someone without cause?

2. How can this verse, coupled with my own experience, give me a greater depth of appreciation of what Christ suffered for me?

Reviewing This Week

Verses   **Personal Application**

Ephesians 1:7

John 1:11-12

Romans 8:38-39

Romans 8:15

John 3:16-17

John 10:28

2 Corinthians 5:21

Day 1—The Joy of Confessing Christ

Memory Verses: Romans 10:9-10

That if you confess with your mouth, "Jesus is Lord," and believe in your heart that God raised him from the dead, you will be saved. For it is with your heart that you believe and are justified, and it is with your mouth that you confess and are saved.

Teena, a college freshman, had just committed her life to Christ, but she was apprehensive about telling anyone—until Bill appeared on the scene. He plunked his coffee cup down on the table and smiled. "I heard something exciting happened to you yesterday, Teena."

"Yeah." Teena paused and looked around, as if seeking an escape route. "I, uh, well, did it."

"Did what?"

"Well, I, ah, gave my life to God."

"That's wonderful!" Bill exclaimed. He was still talking with Teena and encouraging her in her decision when Maria walked by.

"Maria!" Bill called. "Teena wants to tell you something!"

Teena gasped, open-mouthed, then stammered, "I—I committed my life to Christ."

Maria, similarly enthusiastic, encouraged Teena in her commitment, and within half an hour Teena was stopping her friends to tell them, "Guess what? I've become a Christian! I belong to Jesus now!"

Teena had already surrendered her heart to Christ. But when she confessed her decision aloud to others, the truth of that transformation was confirmed in her.

Many of us have been raised to believe that "faith is a private matter," not to be discussed in polite company. Yet Paul makes clear the connection between heart commitment and verbal confession. Just as my love for family and friends deepens as I tell them I love them, so a person's love for Christ is confirmed and stabilized by speaking of that commitment to others.

Application

1. Have I ever been reluctant to tell others of my faith in Christ? Why?

2. What happens within me when I do tell others of my love for the Lord?

Day 2—Alienation and Reconciliation

Memory Verses: Colossians 1:21-22
Once you were alienated from God and were enemies in your minds because of your evil behavior. But now he has reconciled you by Christ's physical body through death to present you holy in his sight, without blemish and free from accusation.

Some fifty years ago, Orson Welles's radio broadcast of *The War of the Worlds* threw the nation into panic; people on the East Coast ran for their lives, expecting at any moment to be destroyed by alien invaders from outer space.

Today, of course, we are more sophisticated about such matters. Television and movies have educated us about alien life forms. *Star Wars* and *Star Trek* have taught us that their appearance can be much different than ours. Sometimes they are unable to exist in our atmosphere without artificial life-support systems; their physical makeup is often incompatible with our environment.

God says that we, apart from Christ, are as incompatible with his kingdom as the "aliens" of movies are with earth's environment. Paul describes us as "alienated from God and . . . enemies in (our) minds." Without the transforming work of the Holy Spirit, we are unable to adapt to his environment. We are at war with God, a true "war of the worlds" that staggers the imagination.

Yet God has "reconciled" us to his world. He has made us fit, made us able to exist in his kingdom. He has made us part of his world through Christ's death and resurrection.

Now, through Christ, we are "holy" and "without blemish" in God's sight. And that transformation, ironically, makes us "alien" in the world around us. No longer do we fit in a world of selfishness and greed, a world where Self is god and everyone does what is right in his own heart. We belong, instead, in the kingdom of God's righteousness.

Application

1. In what ways am I an "alien" in this world?

2. How have I been an "alien" to God's kingdom?

3. How can today's verses help me deal with my sense of "not fitting" in the world?

Day 3—From Darkness to Light

Memory Verses: Colossians 1:13-14

For he has rescued us from the dominion of darkness and brought us into the kingdom of the Son he loves, in whom we have redemption, the forgiveness of sins.

Most of us have no real concept of darkness. We live in a world illuminated not only by sun, moon, and stars, but by streetlights and electric lamps and, when the power goes off, flashlights and candles. We resist the darkness. For the sighted, being in absolute darkness is a frightening experience. The dark blots out everything; we can see nothing, not even our own bodies, and we may become disoriented. The dark seems to press in upon us, with an almost physical weight that oppresses.

Spiritual darkness is like that. Spiritual darkness, the absence of light in Christ, is oppressive, weighing us down, distorting our perceptions of reality. We cannot judge clearly, or we cannot see at all.

Yet God breaks into our darkness, bringing his light—Jesus Christ, the Light of the World. When the awareness of Christ invades our lives, our eyes are opened and we can see for the first time. We see our sin, God's grace, and the Way he has provided for escape from the dark. And as we continue to walk in his light, we see even more—the need for changes in our lives, and God's power to work those changes. Discernment and wisdom come through his light, and we understand spiritual truths we could never see before.

Paul says that God has "rescued" us from darkness and brought us into the light. We cannot, on our own, accomplish this rescue, but God through Christ's sacrifice brings it about in us. He is the light who illuminates our darkness.

Application

1. Many different kinds of spiritual darkness invade our lives and keep us blind to the truth—sin, lack of understanding, resistance to the Holy Spirit. What kinds of spiritual darkness have I experienced?

2. What changes took place in me when I first "came into the light"?

3. What spiritual truths can I see now that I could not see when I lived in darkness?

Day 4—Freedom From Fear

Memory Verse: Psalm 27:1

The Lord is my light and my salvation—whom shall I fear? The Lord is the stronghold of my life—of whom shall I be afraid?

Marcy was afraid of the dark. As a child she slept with a nightlight on, and even as she matured, she still had a fear of dark places. When she was at home alone, she kept all the lights on, and a small lamp at her bedside glowed through the night.

The psalmist David reflects that common fear of darkness when he says, "The Lord is my light and my salvation—whom shall I fear?"

David does not say, "The Lord *brings* light," but "The Lord *is* my light." God is the source of understanding and security in our lives. He is the One who can expose and deal with our fears.

When we are afraid—afraid of losing a job or a loved one, afraid of making mistakes, afraid of being hurt, afraid of what others may say about us—we can turn to the Lord, who can handle our fears. He is a "stronghold," a fortress of protection around us, and in him we are safe.

Often we turn to other places for our security—to the bank account, to a spouse or loved one, to the approval of the world. We mistakenly think that these sources can provide a foundation of defense against the uncertainty of life. But when we find that people disappoint us, money loses its value, and the praise of others is fleeting, we must turn again to the true source of security, God alone.

Application

1. What sources of security have I trusted in besides God? What was the result of that trust?

2. In what ways have I depended upon God for my security?

Week One
Knowing God's Word

I can do everything through him who gives me strength.

Philippians 4:13 (NIV)

How can a young man keep his way pure? By living according to your word. I have hidden your word in my heart that I might not sin against you.

Psalm 119:9, 11 (NIV)

All Scripture is God-breathed and is useful for teaching, rebuking, correcting and training in righteousness, so that the man of God may be thoroughly equipped for every good work.

2 Timothy 3:16-17 (NIV)

Every word of God is flawless; he is a shield to those who take refuge in him.

Proverbs 30:5 (NIV)

Let the word of Christ dwell in you richly as you teach and admonish one another with all wisdom, and as you sing psalms, hymns and spiritual songs with gratitude in your hearts to God.

Colossians 3:16 (NIV)

He taught me and said, "Lay hold of my words with all your heart; keep my commands and you will live. Wisdom is supreme; therefore get wisdom. Though it cost all you have, get understanding."

Proverbs 4:4, 7 (NIV)

Do not let this Book of the Law depart from your mouth; meditate on it day and night, so that you may be careful to do everything written in it. Then you will be prosperous and successful.

Joshua 1:8 (NIV)

I can do all things through Christ which strengtheneth me.

Philippians 4:13 (KJV)

Week One
Knowing God's Word

All scripture is given by inspiration of God, and is profitable for doctrine, for reproof, for correction, for instruction in righteousness: that the man of God may be perfect, thoroughly furnished unto all good works.

2 Timothy 3:16-17 (KJV)

Wherewithal shall a young man cleanse his way? by taking heed thereto according to thy word. With my whole heart have I sought thee: O let me not wander from thy commandments. Thy word have I hid in mine heart, that I might not sin against thee.

Psalm 119:9, 11 (KJV)

Let the word of Christ dwell in you richly in all wisdom; teaching and admonishing one another in psalms and hymns and spiritual songs, singing with grace in your hearts to the Lord.

Colossians 3:16 (KJV)

Every word of God is pure: he is a shield unto them that put their trust in him.

Proverbs 30:5 (KJV)

This book of the law shall not depart out of thy mouth; but thou shalt meditate therein day and night, that thou mayest observe to do according to all that is written therein: for then thou shalt make thy way prosperous, and then thou shalt have good success.

Joshua 1:8 (KJV)

He taught me also, and said unto me, Let thine heart retain my words: keep my commandments, and live. Wisdom is the principal thing; therefore get wisdom: and with all thy getting get understanding.

Proverbs 4:4, 7 (KJV)

Week Two

Saved by Grace

For all have sinned and fall short of the glory of God, and are justified freely by his grace through the redemption that came by Christ Jesus.

Romans 3:23-24 (NIV)

I tell you the truth, whoever hears my word and believes him who sent me has eternal life and will not be condemned; he has crossed over from death to life.

John 5:24 (NIV)

For the wages of sin is death, but the gift of God is eternal life in Christ Jesus our Lord.

Romans 6:23 (NIV)

Therefore, if anyone is in Christ, he is a new creation; the old has gone, the new has come!

2 Corinthians 5:17 (NIV)

Salvation is found in no one else, for there is no other name under heaven given to men by which we must be saved.

Acts 4:12 (NIV)

Therefore, there is now no condemnation for those who are in Christ Jesus, because through Christ Jesus the law of the Spirit of life set me free from the law of sin and death.

Romans 8:1-2 (NIV)

Therefore, my brothers, I want you to know that through Jesus the forgiveness of sins is proclaimed to you.

Acts 13:38 (NIV)

SAVED BY GRACE

For all have sinned, and come short of the glory of God; being justified freely by his grace through the redemption that is in Christ Jesus.

Romans 3:23-24 (KJV)

Week Two
Saved by Grace

SAVED BY GRACE

For the wages of sin is death; but the gift of God is eternal life through Jesus Christ our Lord.

Romans 6:23 (KJV)

SAVED BY GRACE

Verily, verily, I say unto you, He that heareth my word, and believeth on him that sent me, hath everlasting life, and shall not come into condemnation; but is passed from death unto life.

John 5:24 (KJV)

SAVED BY GRACE

Neither is there salvation in any other: for there is none other name under heaven given among men, whereby we must be saved.

Acts 4:12 (KJV)

SAVED BY GRACE

Therefore if any man be in Christ, he is a new creature: old things are passed away; behold, all things are become new.

2 Corinthians 5:17 (KJV)

SAVED BY GRACE

Be it known unto you therefore, men and brethren, that through this man is preached unto you the forgiveness of sins.

Acts 13:38 (KJV)

SAVED BY GRACE

There is therefore now no condemnation to them which are in Christ Jesus, who walk not after the flesh, but after the Spirit. For the law of the Spirit of life in Christ Jesus hath made me free from the law of sin and death.

Romans 8:1-2 (KJV)

Week Three

Saved Now and Forever

In him we have redemption through his blood, the forgiveness of sins, in accordance with the riches of God's grace.

Ephesians 1:7 (NIV)

For God so loved the world that he gave his one and only Son, that whoever believes in him shall not perish but have eternal life. For God did not send his Son into the world to condemn the world, but to save the world through him.

John 3:16-17 (NIV)

He came to that which was his own, but his own did not receive him. Yet to all who received him, to those who believed in his name, he gave the right to become children of God.

John 1:11-12 (NIV)

I give them eternal life, and they shall never perish; no one can snatch them out of my hand.

John 10:28 (NIV)

For I am convinced that neither death nor life, neither angels nor demons, neither the present nor the future, nor any powers, neither height nor depth, nor anything else in all creation, will be able to separate us from the love of God that is in Christ Jesus our Lord.

Romans 8:38-39 (NIV)

God made him who had no sin to be sin for us, so that in him we might become the righteousness of God.

2 Corinthians 5:21 (NIV)

For you did not receive a spirit that makes you a slave again to fear, but you received the Spirit of sonship. And by him we cry, "Abba, Father."

Romans 8:15 (NIV)

In whom we have redemption through his blood, the forgiveness of sins, according to the riches of his grace.

Ephesians 1:7 (KJV)

Week Three

Saved Now and Forever

He came unto his own, and his own received him not. But as many as received him, to them gave he power to become the sons of God, even to them that believe on his name.

John 1:11-12 (KJV)

For God so loved the world, that he gave his only begotten Son, that whosoever believeth in him should not perish, but have everlasting life. For God sent not his Son into the world to condemn the world; but that the world through him might be saved.

John 3:16-17 (KJV)

For I am persuaded, that neither death, nor life, nor angels, nor principalities, nor powers, nor things present, nor things to come, nor height, nor depth, nor any other creature, shall be able to separate us from the love of God, which is in Christ Jesus our Lord.

Romans 8:38-39 (KJV)

And I give unto them eternal life; and they shall never perish, neither shall any man pluck them out of my hand.

John 10:28 (KJV)

For ye have not received the spirit of bondage again to fear; but ye have received the Spirit of adoption, whereby we cry, Abba, Father.

Romans 8:15 (KJV)

For he hath made him to be sin for us, who knew no sin; that we might be made the righteousness of God in him.

2 Corinthians 5:21 (KJV)

Week Four
The Blessings of Grace

That if you confess with your mouth, "Jesus is Lord," and believe in your heart that God raised him from the dead, you will be saved. For it is with your heart that you believe and are justified, and it is with your mouth that you confess and are saved.

Romans 10:9-10 (NIV)

If we confess our sins, he is faithful and just and will forgive us our sins and purify us from all unrighteousness.

1 John 1:9 (NIV)

Once you were alienated from God and were enemies in your minds because of your evil behavior. But now he has reconciled you by Christ's physical body through death to present you holy in his sight, without blemish and free from accusation.

Colossians 1:21-22 (NIV)

"Come now, let us reason together," says the Lord. "Though your sins are like scarlet, they shall be as white as snow; though they are red as crimson, they shall be like wool."

Isaiah 1:18 (NIV)

For he has rescued us from the dominion of darkness and brought us into the kingdom of the Son he loves, in whom we have redemption, the forgiveness of sins.

Colossians 1:13-14 (NIV)

Every valley shall be filled in, every mountain and hill made low. The crooked roads shall become straight, the rough ways smooth. And all mankind will see God's salvation.

Luke 3:5-6 (NIV)

The Lord is my light and my salvation—whom shall I fear? The Lord is the stronghold of my life—of whom shall I be afraid?

Psalm 27:1 (NIV)

That if thou shalt confess with thy mouth the Lord Jesus, and shalt believe in thine heart that God hath raised him from the dead, thou shalt be saved. For with the heart man believeth unto righteousness; and with the mouth confession is made unto salvation.

Romans 10:9-10 (KJV)

Week Four
The Blessings of Grace

THE BLESSINGS OF GRACE

And you, that were sometime alienated and enemies in your mind by wicked works, yet now hath he reconciled in the body of his flesh through death, to present you holy and unblameable and unreproveable in his sight.

Colossians 1:21-22 (KJV)

THE BLESSINGS OF GRACE

If we confess our sins, he is faithful and just to forgive us our sins, and to cleanse us from all unrighteousness.

1 John 1:9 (KJV)

THE BLESSINGS OF GRACE

Who hath delivered us from the power of darkness, and hath translated us into the kingdom of his dear Son: in whom we have redemption through his blood, even the forgiveness of sins.

Colossians 1:13-14 (KJV)

THE BLESSINGS OF GRACE

Come now, and let us reason together, saith the Lord: though your sins be as scarlet, they shall be as white as snow; though they be red like crimson, they shall be as wool.

Isaiah 1:18 (KJV)

THE BLESSINGS OF GRACE

The Lord is my light and my salvation; whom shall I fear? The Lord is the strength of my life; of whom shall I be afraid?

Psalm 27:1 (KJV)

THE BLESSINGS OF GRACE

Every valley shall be filled, and every mountain and hill shall be brought low; and the crooked shall be made straight, and the rough ways shall be made smooth; and all flesh shall see the salvation of God.

Luke 3:5-6 (KJV)

Week Five

Rejoicing in Grace

My God is my rock, in whom I take refuge, my shield and the horn of my salvation. He is my stronghold, my refuge and my savior—from violent men you save me. I call to the Lord, who is worthy of praise, and I am saved from my enemies.

2 Samuel 22:3-4 (NIV)

But now, this is what the Lord says— he who created you, O Jacob, he who formed you, O Israel: "Fear not, for I have redeemed you; I have summoned you by name; you are mine."

Isaiah 43:1 (NIV)

I delight greatly in the Lord; my soul rejoices in my God. For he has clothed me with garments of salvation and arrayed me in a robe of righteousness, as a bridegroom adorns his head like a priest, and as a bride adorns herself with her jewels.

Isaiah 61:10 (NIV)

Therefore, my dear friends, as you have always obeyed—not only in my presence, but now much more in my absence—continue to work out your salvation with fear and trembling, for it is God who works in you to will and to act according to his good purpose.

Philippians 2:12-13 (NIV)

The Lord is my strength and my song; he has become my salvation. He is my God, and I will praise him, my father's God, and I will exalt him.

Exodus 15:2 (NIV)

Sow for yourselves righteousness, reap the fruit of unfailing love, and break up your unplowed ground; for it is time to seek the Lord, until he comes and showers righteousness on you.

Hosea 10:12 (NIV)

But I trust in your unfailing love; my heart rejoices in your salvation. I will sing to the Lord, for he has been good to me.

Psalm 13:5-6 (NIV)

REJOICING IN GRACE

The God of my rock; in him will I trust: he is my shield, and the horn of my salvation, my high tower, and my refuge, my saviour; thou savest me from violence. I will call on the Lord, who is worthy to be praised: so shall I be saved from mine enemies.

2 Samuel 22:3-4 (KJV)

Week Five
Rejoicing in Grace

REJOICING IN GRACE

I will greatly rejoice in the Lord, my soul shall be joyful in my God; for he hath clothed me with the garments of salvation, he hath covered me with the robe of righteousness, as a bridegroom decketh himself with ornaments, and as a bride adorneth herself with her jewels.

Isaiah 61:10 (KJV)

REJOICING IN GRACE

But now thus saith the Lord that created thee, O Jacob, and he that formed thee, O Israel, Fear not: for I have redeemed thee, I have called thee by thy name; thou art mine.

Isaiah 43:1 (KJV)

REJOICING IN GRACE

The Lord is my strength and song, and he is become my salvation: he is my God, and I will prepare him an habitation; my father's God, and I will exalt him.

Exodus 15:2 (KJV)

REJOICING IN GRACE

Wherefore, my beloved, as ye have always obeyed, not as in my presence only, but now much more in my absence, work out your own salvation with fear and trembling. For it is God which worketh in you both to will and to do of his good pleasure.

Philippians 2:12-13 (KJV)

REJOICING IN GRACE

But I have trusted in thy mercy; my heart shall rejoice in thy salvation. I will sing unto the Lord, because he hath dealt bountifully with me.

Psalm 13:5-6 (KJV)

REJOICING IN GRACE

Sow to yourselves in righteousness, reap in mercy; break up your fallow ground: for it is time to seek the Lord, till he come and rain righteousness upon you.

Hosea 10:12 (KJV)

Week Six

Showing Grace to Others

Bear with each other and forgive whatever grievances you may have against one another. Forgive as the Lord forgave you.

Colossians 3:13 (NIV)

SHOWING GRACE TO OTHERS

And when you stand praying, if you hold anything against anyone, forgive him, so that your Father in heaven may forgive you your sins.

Mark 11:25 (NIV)

SHOWING GRACE TO OTHERS

For if you forgive men when they sin against you, your heavenly Father will also forgive you. But if you do not forgive men their sins, your Father will not forgive your sins.

Matthew 6:14-15 (NIV)

SHOWING GRACE TO OTHERS

All this is from God, who reconciled us to himself through Christ and gave us the ministry of reconciliation: that God was reconciling the world to himself in Christ, not counting men's sins against them. And he has committed to us the message of reconciliation.

2 Corinthians 5:18-19 (NIV)

SHOWING GRACE TO OTHERS

Be kind and compassionate to one another, forgiving each other, just as in Christ God forgave you.

Ephesians 4:32 (NIV)

SHOWING GRACE TO OTHERS

How beautiful on the mountains are the feet of those who bring good news, who proclaim peace, who bring good tidings, who proclaim salvation, who say to Zion, "Your God reigns!"

Isaiah 52:7 (NIV)

SHOWING GRACE TO OTHERS

So watch yourselves. If your brother sins, rebuke him, and if he repents, forgive him. If he sins against you seven times in a day, and seven times comes back to you and says, "I repent," forgive him.

Luke 17:3-4 (NIV)

Forbearing one another, and forgiving one another, if any man have a quarrel against any: even as Christ forgave you, so also do ye.

Colossians 3:13 (KJV)

Week Six
Showing Grace to Others

For if ye forgive men their trespasses, your heavenly Father will also forgive you: but if ye forgive not men their trespasses, neither will your Father forgive your trespasses.

Matthew 6:14-15 (KJV)

And when ye stand praying, forgive, if ye have aught against any: that your Father also which is in heaven may forgive you your trespasses.

Mark 11:25 (KJV)

And be ye kind one to another, tenderhearted, forgiving one another, even as God for Christ's sake hath forgiven you.

Ephesians 4:32 (KJV)

And all things are of God, who hath reconciled us to himself by Jesus Christ, and hath given to us the ministry of reconciliation; to wit, that God was in Christ, reconciling the world unto himself, not imputing their trespasses unto them; and hath committed unto us the word of reconciliation.

2 Corinthians 5:18-19 (KJV)

Take heed to yourselves: If thy brother trespass against thee, rebuke him; and if he repent, forgive him. And if he trespass against thee seven times in a day, and seven times in a day turn again to thee, saying, I repent; thou shalt forgive him.

Luke 17:3-4 (KJV)

How beautiful upon the mountains are the feet of him that bringeth good tidings, that publisheth peace; that bringeth good tidings of good, that publisheth salvation; that saith unto Zion, Thy God reigneth!

Isaiah 52:7 (KJV)

Week Seven
Promises of Grace

Therefore I tell you, whatever you ask for in prayer, believe that you have received it, and it will be yours.

Mark 11:24 (NIV)

No temptation has seized you except what is common to man. And God is faithful; he will not let you be tempted beyond what you can bear. But when you are tempted, he will also provide a way out so that you can stand up under it.

1 Corinthians 10:13 (NIV)

Let us not become weary in doing good, for at the proper time we will reap a harvest if we do not give up.

Galatians 6:9 (NIV)

Humble yourselves, therefore, under God's mighty hand, that he may lift you up in due time. Cast all your anxiety on him because he cares for you.

1 Peter 5:6-7 (NIV)

And my God will meet all your needs according to his glorious riches in Christ Jesus.

Philippians 4:19 (NIV)

The eternal God is your refuge, and underneath are the everlasting arms. He will drive out your enemy before you, saying, "Destroy him!"

Deuteronomy 33:27 (NIV)

Give, and it will be given to you. A good measure, pressed down, shaken together and running over, will be poured into your lap. For with the measure you use, it will be measured to you.

Luke 6:38 (NIV)

Therefore I say unto you, What things soever ye desire, when ye pray, believe that ye receive them, and ye shall have them.

Mark 11:24 (KJV)

Week Seven
Promises of Grace

And let us not be weary in well doing: for in due season we shall reap, if we faint not.

Galatians 6:9 (KJV)

There hath no temptation taken you but such as is common to man: but God is faithful, who will not suffer you to be tempted above that ye are able; but will with the temptation also make a way to escape, that ye may be able to bear it.

1 Corinthians 10:13 (KJV)

But my God shall supply all your need according to his riches in glory by Christ Jesus.

Philippians 4:19 (KJV)

Humble yourselves therefore under the mighty hand of God, that he may exalt you in due time: casting all your care upon him; for he careth for you.

1 Peter 5:6-7 (KJV)

Give, and it shall be given unto you; good measure, pressed down, and shaken together, and running over, shall men give into your bosom. For with the same measure that ye mete withal it shall be measured to you again.

Luke 6:38 (KJV)

The eternal God is thy refuge, and underneath are the everlasting arms: and he shall thrust out the enemy from before thee; and shall say, Destroy them.

Deuteronomy 33:27 (KJV)

Week Eight
Guided by Grace

When Jesus spoke again to the people, he said, "I am the light of the world. Whoever follows me will never walk in darkness, but will have the light of life."

John 8:12 (NIV)

But those who hope in the Lord will renew their strength. They will soar on wings like eagles; they will run and not grow weary, they will walk and not be faint.

Isaiah 40:31 (NIV)

And we know that in all things God works for the good of those who love him, who have been called according to his purpose. For those God foreknew he also predestined to be conformed to the likeness of his Son, that he might be the firstborn among many brothers.

Romans 8:28-29 (NIV)

When you pass through the waters, I will be with you; and when you pass through the rivers, they will not sweep over you. When you walk through the fire, you will not be burned; the flames will not set you ablaze.

Isaiah 43:2 (NIV)

Being confident of this, that he who began a good work in you will carry it on to completion until the day of Christ Jesus.

Philippians 1:6 (NIV)

So do not fear, for I am with you; do not be dismayed, for I am your God. I will strengthen you and help you; I will uphold you with my righteous right hand.

Isaiah 41:10 (NIV)

If any of you lacks wisdom, he should ask God, who gives generously to all without finding fault, and it will be given to him.

James 1:5 (NIV)

Then spake Jesus again unto them, saying, I am the light of the world: he that followeth me shall not walk in darkness, but shall have the light of life.

John 8:12 (KJV)

Week Eight
Guided by Grace

And we know that all things work together for good to them that love God, to them who are the called according to his purpose. For whom he did foreknow, he also did predestinate to be conformed to the image of his Son, that he might be the firstborn among many brethren.

Romans 8:28-29 (KJV)

But they that wait upon the Lord shall renew their strength; they shall mount up with wings as eagles; they shall run, and not be weary; and they shall walk, and not faint.

Isaiah 40:31 (KJV)

Being confident of this very thing, that he which hath begun a good work in you will perform it until the day of Jesus Christ.

Philippians 1:6 (KJV)

When thou passest through the waters, I will be with thee; and through the rivers, they shall not overflow thee: when thou walkest through the fire, thou shalt not be burned; neither shall the flame kindle upon thee.

Isaiah 43:2 (KJV)

If any of you lack wisdom, let him ask of God, that giveth to all men liberally, and upbraideth not; and it shall be given him.

James 1:5 (KJV)

Fear thou not; for I am with thee: be not dismayed; for I am thy God: I will strengthen thee; yea, I will help thee; yea, I will uphold thee with the right hand of my righteousness.

Isaiah 41:10 (KJV)

Day 5—Why Confess?

Memory Verse: 1 John 1:9
If we confess our sins, he is faithful and just and will forgive us our sins and purify us from all unrighteousness.

"If God already knows everything about me, everything I've done, then why do I need to confess it?" Grant struggled with a common dilemma for many Christians. Indeed, God knew all his sin—much better than Grant did himself. But Grant needed to confess, not for God's benefit, but for his own. Grant needed to agree with God that his sin was wrong, and put himself in a position to receive God's grace in forgiveness.

1 John 1:9 makes the process quite clear. We *confess,* and God *forgives* and *cleanses*. Many of us, however, want to take on God's part as well. We confess, agreeing with God that our sin is wrong. But then we proceed to try to "clean up our act," bargaining with God, promising that if he will forgive us just this once, we won't ever do it again.

The problem is, we can never keep such a promise. We probably will do it again, and then we are back where we started, begging for forgiveness, and trying once more to cleanse ourselves from our unrighteousness.

God offers freedom from such futile performance. He says, "Just confess. Agree that you sinned. Submit yourself to me. Then I'll take over from there." God's grace does not give us freedom to keep on sinning, of course—we need to cooperate with the work of his Spirit in our lives and do all we can to avoid sin. But we do not have to beg God for forgiveness—forgiveness is offered to us freely.

We do not have to clean up our act before God will accept us; God can make the necessary changes in our lives. When we confess, submit ourselves to God, and allow him to work within us, he is able both to forgive us and to cleanse us from unrighteousness.

Application

1. In what ways have I bartered with God and tried to "clean up my act" in order to deserve his forgiveness?

2. What is my part in confession? What is God's response? Why is it important for me to recognize God's part in my confession and forgiveness?

Day 6—A Reasonable Alternative

Memory Verse: Isaiah 1:18
"Come now, let us reason together," says the Lord. "Though your sins are like scarlet, they shall be as white as snow; though they are red as crimson, they shall be like wool."

"Is Christianity reasonable?" Linda wanted to know. "I've heard all my life that faith is a crutch, an invention of weak minds to assure them of some order in the world." Linda was not alone in her objection; thinking people for generations have been asking themselves the same question.

God is not intimidated by our questions; in fact, he confronts the issue head-on in the Scriptures. "Let us reason together," the Lord invites. Even according to the most basic of human reasoning, faith is a reasonable alternative, a rational choice for a thinking person.

God indicates in his Word that confession and forgiveness are "reasonable." "Think!" God says. "You sin, and you know it. You aren't even able to be true to your own principles. You cannot deal with your sin by will power or effort. But I can deal with it! I can forgive it—and I will."

We cannot come to faith in God through Christ by intellect alone, of course. Our spirits must reach out in faith, beyond what we can see. But intellect supports faith; trusting in Christ is an eminently rational decision.

In Deuteronomy 30:19-20, God sets before the people a choice: life or death, blessing or cursing. "Choose life!" he tells them. We have the same choice. The ultimate decision is the choice between life and death—and when the decision is thus simplified, the "rational" alternative becomes clear. We can choose death, by attempting to control our own destinies, or life, by giving ourselves fully into the hands of the Master.

Application

1. Why is the choice to acknowledge my sin and receive forgiveness a "rational choice"?

2. What are the alternatives to such a decision?

3. What other aspects of God's Word and work in my life seem "reasonable" to me?

Day 7—God's Bulldozer

Memory Verses: Luke 3:5-6

Every valley shall be filled in, every mountain and hill made low. The crooked roads shall become straight, the rough ways smooth. And all mankind will see God's salvation.

When a new highway is being constructed, the road crews work hard in preparing for the new surface to be laid. Giant bulldozers cut through the hillsides, moving earth, leveling, filling, evening out the path where the roadway will run. When the work is first begun, it often looks like chaos: and even after the highway begins to take shape, the land is still ugly, scarred by the unsightly gashes cut through the landscape. Yet after the work is completed and the grass and trees are replanted, we forget the temporary upheaval and see only the beauty of the land and the convenience of the new roadway.

In Luke 3:5-6, John the Baptist presents a prophecy of the coming of Christ, a prophecy quoted from Isaiah 40:3-5. The prophecy speaks of the preparation of the world for the coming Messiah, but it also applies to the preparation of the individual heart to receive him.

Sometimes, the Holy Spirit must do major work in our hearts to prepare us for the coming of Christ into our lives. Like a bulldozer, he brings down the mountains of pride in our lives. He fills the empty places, corrects the crooked, grades down the rough edges of our hearts.

Often this is not pleasant work. We prefer to maintain the rugged landscape of Self, and we do not like the ugly scars that are left after the bulldozer has done its job. But if we submit to the Spirit's "construction work" in us, the way will be paved for the Lord to enter into our lives, and others will see in us the glory and salvation of our God.

Application

1. What "construction work" has the Holy Spirit done in me?

2. What restoration has taken place because of that work?

3. How do today's verses help me put in perspective the work God still wants to do in me?

Reviewing This Week

Verses   **Personal Application**

Romans 10:9-10

Colossians 1:21-22

Colossians 1:13-14

Psalm 27:1

1 John 1:9

Isaiah 1:18

Luke 3:5-6

Day 1—Call to the Lord

Memory Verses: 2 Samuel 22:3-4

My God is my rock, in whom I take refuge, my shield and the horn of my salvation. He is my stronghold, my refuge and my savior—from violent men you save me. I call to the Lord, who is worthy of praise, and I am saved from my enemies.

In the old days of television westerns, we could always tell who the enemy was. The bad guys wore black hats; the evil villain had a scar across his cheek or a patch over one eye. But real life is not quite so simple. Enemies come in many forms, and often are not easy to recognize. Sin is an enemy; even those we love can seek to undermine our faith; modern materialism and distorted values lead us away from biblical principles. These enemies may not seek our death in a physical sense, but their influence results in spiritual death or, at the very least, immaturity.

Yet God promises to rescue us from our enemies. David describes the Lord as a "rock," a "shield," a "stronghold," and a "refuge." God provides a stable foundation for our faith; he protects us from the attacks of the Enemy; he offers a place of rest in the battle.

Our battles are usually not physical ones, but rather spiritual and emotional wars. We struggle with difficult relationships, the burdens of the past, the subtle accusations of the devil.

But these enemies can be overcome. David says, "I call to the Lord, *who is worthy of praise*" (italics added). When we turn to the Lord, trust his Word, acknowledge his worthiness, we put our own problems and difficulties in perspective. We see that God is able to rescue us, and has promised to do so. And as we respond to his grace by focusing on him, we abandon trust in ourselves and allow him to do what he has promised.

Application

1. What kinds of enemies do I face?

2. How have I tried to deal with those enemies by myself?

3. How can today's verses help me turn to the source of my rescue?

Day 2—The Wardrobe of Joy

Memory Verse: Isaiah 61:10

I delight greatly in the Lord; my soul rejoices in my God. For he has clothed me with garments of salvation and arrayed me in a robe of righteousness, as a bridegroom adorns his head like a priest, and as a bride adorns herself with her jewels.

On her wedding day, the bride dresses carefully for the ceremony that is about to take place. Never before has she spent so much time in preparation for one relatively brief event. When she looks in the mirror and rejoices in her happiness, she responds not out of vanity, but for sheer joy as she anticipates the coming ceremony.

God wants his people, like that bride, to be joyful, to rejoice in the Lord, the Bridegroom. And he gives, through his grace, the garments of joy to his beloved ones. He clothes us, Isaiah says, with salvation, and covers us with the robe of righteousness.

The wardrobe that God provides is not merely a utility garment, a coverall that hides our sin from his eyes. It is his own righteousness in Christ, given to us as a free gift, so that we might be united with him. And God himself, Isaiah says, is filled with joy, adorning himself like a bridegroom.

When we truly see God's immeasurable gift in accepting us as his own, we also will "greatly rejoice" in the Lord. He, the eternal God, Creator of the universe, desires to be united with us, as a husband desires his wife! God does not simply accept us grudgingly, reminding us of our unworthiness to be with him. Rather, he celebrates with unrestrained joy his oneness in Spirit with those he calls his own. And we, having been fully forgiven and set free from sin, can rejoice unashamedly as well.

Application

1. Have I ever felt ashamed to draw close to God? Why?

2. What does this verse tell me about God's attitude toward me?

Day 3—The Song of Exaltation

Memory Verse: Exodus 15:2
The Lord is my strength and my song; he has become my salvation. He is my God, and I will praise him, my father's God, and I will exalt him.

The world is full of music that communicates human emotion: love, joy, sadness, separation. A love song makes us misty-eyed; a song of protest arouses anger; a song describing loss stimulates feelings of hurt and abandonment. Music is a powerful force to sway the human spirit.

Exodus 15:2 indicates that God should be the source of the songs in our hearts. Human emotions vacillate; human relationships disappoint, but God is our "strength" and our "song."

To exalt the Lord includes many different types of "songs." "I can't carry a tune in a bucket," one woman complained. "How can I sing to the Lord anything that will be pleasing to him?" But the Lord does not delight in the professionalism of our songs, but in the motivation of our hearts. We can "sing to the Lord" when we enjoy a Bach organ piece played for his glory. We can exalt him in the words of Scripture—either remembered or sung. We can worship him by enjoying the songs of others.

The key to making the Lord our song is exaltation. When our thoughts lift him up in praise, we are singing a song of exaltation to the Lord.

When God is exalted in our songs, in our hearts, and in our thoughts, that focus gives strength to our lives. We can face the difficulties that are an inevitable part of human experience, because God is our "strength and our song."

Application

1. What is the difference between a song that is professionally performed and one that exalts the Lord?

2. What practical steps can I take to make my daily life a "song of praise" to God?

Day 4—Under the Mercy

Memory Verses: Psalm 13:5-6
But I trust in your unfailing love; my heart rejoices in your salvation. I will sing to the Lord, for he has been good to me.

In Sheldon Vanauken's book *A Severe Mercy,* Vanauken faced the "severe mercy" of the untimely death of his wife. His friend C. S. Lewis, who had endured a similar grief, comforted him through letters, encouraging him with the exhortation, "Go under the mercy."

While God's grace deals with sin and forgiveness, God's mercy deals with the pain of human existence. We all experience pain—sometimes as a natural result of wrongs we have done, sometimes unfairly as a consequence of living in a fallen world. But for all who hurt, God provides mercy—respite from pain, and the assurance of a Lord who cares.

David, in Psalm 13 says, "I trust in your mercy, your unfailing love." God's love never fails us, no matter how much we may have failed him. David knew the consequences of sin; he knew what it meant to fail God, to rebel against God's faithfulness. Yet David trusted in God's goodness rather than depending upon his own; he focused his attention upon the mercy of the Lord.

We need, like David, to "go under the mercy," even when it is a "severe mercy." Even when circumstances seem bad; even when things seem out of control; even when we think God has forsaken us, yet his mercy is at work to bring us fulfillment and cause us to turn to him with a song of praise on our lips.

Application

1. How have I experienced the mercy of God?

2. How can these verses help me focus on God's merciful intervention in my life even when circumstances seem out of control?

Day 5—Called by Name

Memory Verse: Isaiah 43:1

But now, this is what the Lord says—he who created you, O Jacob, he who formed you, O Israel: "Fear not, for I have redeemed you; I have summoned you by name; you are mine."

Eric, age four, somehow lost his mother in a large and busy department store. Found sobbing under a coat rack, the boy tried to tell the security guard where he was when he got separated from his mother. Finally the guard said, "What's your name, Son? Who do you belong to?" The child brightened a bit, gave the guard his name, and within minutes the frantic mother was reunited with her lost son.

One of the first questions we are asked, both as children and adults, is "What is your name?"—that is, "Whose are you? Who do you belong to?" Children bear the name of their parents, and most women, except for professional reasons, take the name of their husbands when they marry. Our names are our primary method of identification; they connect us with our heritage and with those we love.

In Isaiah 43:1, God declares that we belong to him. The Lord who created us and formed us says, "I have redeemed you; I have called you by name; you are mine." God's right of ownership in our lives extends beyond the bond of family and friends, of parent, child, or spouse. We belong first to him; we are called by him into oneness with him.

The Scripture is filled with images of the Lord's care for us; when we are lost, he does not wait for us to find him, but takes the initiative, like a loving parent to seek us out. That declaration of belonging can give us a strong sense of security in our lives. God loves us; he will never let us go.

Application

1. What experiences have I had of being lost or abandoned?

2. How can today's verse help me find security in belonging to God?

Day 6—God Works!

Memory Verses: Philippians 2:12-13
Therefore, my dear friends, as you have always obeyed—not only in my presence, but now much more in my absence—continue to work out your salvation with fear and trembling, for it is God who works in you to will and to act according to his good purpose.

"I just can't do it!" Marlys, a career woman in her thirties, was struggling to fit her new Christian principles into the business world. Accustomed to the cutthroat tactics of the corporate hierarchy, she had a hard time knowing how Jesus' examples of grace and mercy applied.

Marlys was right. She couldn't do it. In our own strength, none of us is able to "live the Christian life." Someone has said, "The Christian life isn't difficult—it's impossible!" Only the power of the Holy Spirit is effective to work the needed changes in our priorities and behavior; only God can accomplish what he calls us to do.

In Philippians 2:12, Paul says "work it out." If we stop there, we are likely to throw up our hands in despair. But the good news appears in verse 13: "For it is *God who works in you* to will and to act according to his good purpose" (italics added).

We are not left on our own to figure out how to live the Christian life. God gives us both the *will* and the *ability* to obey him, to live in a way that will please him.

The key to a God-pleasing life is not *performance*, but *obedience.* God does not expect us to "do great things" for him, to deserve his love and grace. Our part in the process of salvation is to respond in obedience to the Lord, to say "yes" to what he asks of us. We cannot change ourselves; we cannot even know ourselves apart from the Spirit's insight. But as we cooperate with him, as we agree to be obedient, the Spirit changes us within, and those changes are "worked out" into our lives.

Application

1. Have I ever tried to "live the Christian life" on my own strength? What was the result?

2. In what practical ways is Paul's declaration that "God works in me" *good news* in my life?

Day 7—Break Up Your Fallow Ground

Memory Verse: Hosea 10:12

Sow for yourselves righteousness, reap the fruit of unfailing love, and break up your unplowed ground; for it is time to seek the Lord, until he comes and showers righteousness on you.

When a farmer prepares to plant his crop, a great deal of preparation is necessary before the seed can be sown. He has to plow up the ground, turning under the stubble from the previous harvest, harrow the field to break up the clods, and fertilize—readying the soil for optimum growth. A fallow field, one that was not planted the previous season, must be broken and worked so that the seed can find root in the ground.

The Bible likens spiritual growth to raising crops. God is the one who brings the rain and gives the growth, but the success or failure of the seed—both in initial salvation and in ongoing maturity—is often linked to how well the soil has been prepared.

That preparation isn't always a pleasant or rewarding process. We may resist the plowing or harrowing that comes through the Holy Spirit's conviction of sin. We may need to dig up boulders of bitterness and thistles of anger; we may have to plow under the stubble of the last crop of lessons, working that mulch deep into our lives.

But the final outcome is worth the effort—even the pain—that preparation brings. Broken up, harrowed, readied for the seed of God's Word, we are rich and fertile ground, and the seed of righteousness produces an abundant crop in us.

Application

1. In what ways have I been "broken up" and "harrowed" by the Holy Spirit to prepare me for God's work in me?

2. How can I apply these verses to myself? How can I "sow in righteousness," "reap in mercy," "break up my fallow ground"?

Reviewing This Week

Verses   **Personal Application**

2 Samuel 22:3-4

Isaiah 61:10

Exodus 15:2

Psalm 13:5-6

Isaiah 43:1

Philippians 2:12-13

Hosea 10:12

Day 1—Forgiving as God Forgave

Memory Verse: Colossians 3:13
Bear with each other and forgive whatever grievances you may have against one another. Forgive as the Lord forgave you.

"No!" Brett slammed his hand against the desk to punctuate his point. "My wife's infidelity is completely unforgivable. She just wants to make things look good, to have me condone her new relationship. I won't do it. I won't forgive her."

Brett was a man in pain, and his perspective on forgiving his wife is understandable. But unfortunately, many of us are the victims of "unforgivable" offenses; many of us, as well, are the perpetrators of such offenses, and we desperately need to be forgiven.

Brett ultimately came to understand that forgiving an "unforgivable" hurt is not based on the worthiness of the recipient of the forgiveness, but on the worthiness of Christ himself. The Bible teaches that we are bound to forgiveness for one simple reason: *because God has forgiven us in Christ.*

"Forgive as the Lord forgave," Paul commands in Colossians 3:13. How did Christ forgive? Freely, completely, without basing his forgiveness on our merit or deserving. He forgave us unilaterally, offering forgiveness *before* we asked, *before* we were aware of our sin and the pain it caused him, *before* we came to him in repentance.

Forgiveness does more than release the perpetrator from the bondage of his wrongdoing. It releases the victim as well. Forgiveness frees the forgiver from the bondage of anger and bitterness that keeps him distant from the love of God. We can forgive the most "unforgivable" of offenses against us when we focus our attention not on the offender, but on Christ, who forgave us.

Application

1. Have I ever harbored unforgiveness toward another person? What was the result in my spiritual/emotional life?

2. Is there someone in my life who has hurt me, whom I need to forgive? How can this verse help me extend forgiveness to that person?

Day 2—The Key to the Prison Cell

Memory Verses: Matthew 6:14-15

For if you forgive men when they sin against you, your heavenly Father will also forgive you. But if you do not forgive men their sins, your Father will not forgive your sins.

Ann had been badly wounded in a relationship that had ended in anger and accusation. For more than a year, Ann nursed her bitterness, rallying support for her attitudes from friends and colleagues. Any time she saw her former friend, Ann put up an icy wall of hostility. She thought she was "getting over" the hurt, but the very mention of her friend's name brought back a flood of negative feelings. Ann was trapped, locked in a prison of unforgiveness, a jail built block by block by her own unwillingness to forgive. Ann didn't "get over it"; instead, her wounds festered and her bitterness grew worse.

Then one day—she never knew how—Ann let go of her bitterness. The barriers of hostility and anger melted away, and when she saw her friend again, she was able to forgive. And Ann was finally able to turn to the Lord for her own healing and forgiveness.

"If you do not forgive," Jesus says—and the statement falls hard on unforgiving hearts, "neither will you be forgiven." In one sense, God's forgiveness is unconditional—we do not have to earn or deserve it, and it is always available to us. But we cannot experience the forgiveness God has extended to us when we harbor unforgiveness towards others and build walls of bitterness in our hearts.

When we refuse forgiveness toward those who have hurt or betrayed us, we do not keep *them* in bondage, but *ourselves*. We lock ourselves away from an awareness of God's loving presence; we imprison ourselves in a cell of revenge. But when we reach out to forgive, we turn the key in the lock; the door is open for our own sins to be forgiven and our own hearts cleansed and purified.

Application

1. Why is forgiving others a condition for experiencing forgiveness in my own life?

2. How can these verses have a practical effect upon my willingness to forgive others?

Day 3—The Kind Heart of Forgiveness

Memory Verse: Ephesians 4:32

Be kind and compassionate to one another, forgiving each other, just as in Christ God forgave you.

Don had lost his job because he stood against his boss and refused to compromise his Christian principles. Certain friends in the company had turned against him, choosing to save their own jobs at any cost, and he felt very alone, abandoned when he most needed the support of those who cared.

But Don showed no signs of bitterness or unforgiveness. He refused to recite the details of his firing to those around him, saying simply and honestly, "I believe my boss was wrong in what he did. But God can show him." The kindness of Don's heart, and the tenderness with which he extended forgiveness, became a testimony to all who knew him. Don's boss never "saw the light," never repented, but Don lived in the freedom of forgiving.

Compassion is a rare commodity among Christians today. We seem to be overstocked with judgment and crammed full of condemnation, but we have little space in the corners of our lives for tenderheartedness. We are quick to assume that we know another person's heart and have the remedy for the problem, rather than giving that person the benefit of the doubt, the room to grow, the freedom to make a mistake and seek forgiveness.

Jesus demonstrated the kind of compassion necessary in forgiveness when he looked down at the soldiers who had crucified him, gambling at his feet for his cloak, and said, "Father, forgive them, for they do not know what they are doing."

When others hurt and betray us, they often "do not know what they are doing." We can, in Christ, offer compassionate forgiveness to them—not condoning their actions or excusing their wrong, but forgiving, in the simplicity and purity of God's love.

Application

1. What is the difference between *excusing* a wrong and *forgiving*?

2. How has God forgiven me for Christ's sake?

3. What does today's verse tell me about my *attitude* in forgiveness?

Day 4—"Formula" for Forgiveness

Memory Verses: Luke 17:3-4

So watch yourselves. If your brother sins, rebuke him, and if he repents, forgive him. If he sins against you seven times in a day, and seven times comes back to you and says, "I repent," forgive him.

The context of these verses give us an interesting perspective of Jesus' disciples. In a corollary passage in Matthew 18, the disciples (through Peter, the designated mouthpiece) ask Jesus, "Lord, how many times shall I forgive my brother when he sins against me?" (Matthew 18:21)

The disciples wanted a "formula" for forgiveness; they wanted to be able to develop a checklist. Once, twice, maybe three times a brother could be forgiven, but after that, you could write him off. After all, if he keeps on offending over and over again, he doesn't *deserve* to be forgiven!

But Jesus says, "Rebuke him—let him know his fault; if he repents, forgive him—even seven times in the same day!"

And the disciples' response is predictable: "Lord, increase our faith!" They were more comfortable with their own formula for forgiveness than with the outrageous demands of love that Christ imposed upon them.

We are so like the disciples. We want to draw a line and say, "This far—no more. I'll forgive you once, but don't do it again. Now that you're forgiven, you'd better shape up!" Yet God's love doesn't recognize "again." He forgives, and no matter how often we come to him in repentance for repeated offenses, his arms of forgiveness are open to us.

That is the way God wants us to forgive. He wants us to lay aside our checklists, put away our suspicions, abandon our scorecards, and forgive. Seven times, or seventy times seven, as often as we have sinned against God and been forgiven, we are to forgive.

Application

1. Have I ever kept a "scorecard" of performance on someone I have forgiven? Why?

2. Why do I need "increased faith" to be able to forgive as Jesus calls me to?

Day 5—When You Pray

Memory Verse: Mark 11:25
And when you stand praying, if you hold anything against anyone, forgive him, so that your Father in heaven may forgive you your sins.

My prayers don't seem to be very effective," a man told his pastor. "I try to make contact with God, but my prayers seem to hit the ceiling and bounce back."

The pastor thought for a moment, then gently suggested, "Is there someone in your life you haven't forgiven?"

"What do you mean?" The man's face flushed; the pastor had obviously struck a nerve. "Well, I guess I've had some struggles with my mother . . . and then, my wife and I . . . " The hidden truth came to light: the man was bound in unforgiving relationships with five of the closest people to him.

Forgiveness is an essential element in prayer. For a very good reason, worship services in liturgical churches place the confession of sin and the absolution near the beginning of the service, before the reading of God's Word, prayer, and the sermon. Forgiveness—both the Lord's forgiveness of us and our forgiveness of others—clears the way for unhindered communication between God and his people.

When we carry anger and bitterness, or even deeply buried, well-sublimated unforgiveness, into the presence of God, our prayers will be affected. We can, however, free the Holy Spirit to work in our lives and the lives of others through forgiveness. We can choose to forgive in light of God's forgiveness of us. And when we do, the channels are re-established; we can pray in power and open ourselves to an awareness of his activity in our lives.

Application

1. Have my prayers ever been affected by unforgiveness in my life?

2. Is there someone in my life whom I need to forgive, whether or not I can work toward reconciliation?

Day 6—Reconciliation

Memory Verses: 2 Corinthians 5:18-19
All this is from God, who reconciled us to himself through Christ and gave us the ministry of reconciliation: that God was reconciling the world to himself in Christ, not counting men's sins against them. And he has committed to us the message of reconciliation.

When Paul writes in 2 Corinthians 5:17 that we become a "new creation" in Christ Jesus, the story does not end there. The verses following give us direction for that new life in Christ. "All this," Paul says, referring to the miracle of new life in Christ, "is from God, who reconciled us to himself through Christ and gave us the ministry of reconciliation."

Reconciliation means to bring back together what was once separated. Man was separated from God by sin, and God took the initiative to reconcile man to himself. Our "ministry of reconciliation" as Christians is twofold: to draw others to the Lord and to work for reconciliation between individuals.

Reconciliation is the ultimate goal of forgiveness. God, through his grace, extends forgiveness to us when we are still sinners, unrepentant, undeserving. When we respond, we come into reconciliation with him and are brought back into oneness. Likewise, when we extend the grace of forgiveness to another, we are set free by the act of forgiving, but we hope that the ultimate outcome will be reconciliation.

God shows us the pattern: he is the wronged party, yet he does not wait for the offender to come to him, hat in hand. He takes a bold initiative, offering forgiveness freely without regard to merit. The pattern applies to us; as the new life in Christ takes hold of us, we must reach out, and reach, and keep on reaching, breaking down the barriers, taking the risk of rejection so that we may come to reconciliation.

Application

1. What barriers stand between me and reconciliation with another person?

2. How can I take a risk and reach out to offer forgiveness and reconciliation to them?

3. What kind of attitude do I need to be a "minister of reconciliation"?

Day 7—Our God Reigns!

Memory Verse: Isaiah 52:7
How beautiful on the mountains are the feet of those who bring good news, who proclaim peace, who bring good tidings, who proclaim salvation, who say to Zion, "Your God reigns!"

A messenger has a single duty: to carry information. During World War II, many parents dreaded the arrival of the Western Union messenger, believing that the delivery of a telegram meant that their son had been wounded or killed.

Isaiah 52:7, however, indicates that a messenger's word is not always unwelcome. "How beautiful on the mountains are the feet of those who bring good news. . . ." the prophet says. The "good news"? *Peace, salvation*, and the resultant message: *"Your God reigns!"*

Our God reigns—in forgiveness, in reconciliation, bringing peace and freedom and joy. Our God reigns, controlling our lives with a loving hand, ordering our experiences for our good, and for his glory. Our God reigns in relationships, in professional circumstances, in families, in churches. The good news is proclaimed: *life is not unmanageable. Our God reigns!*

When we know that God reigns in our lives, we can relax, let go of the reins of control, and live in peace. We can forgive those who have hurt us, knowing that God will reveal to them what they need to know. We can live with good times and bad, recognizing that God uses every circumstance of our lives to conform us to the image of his Son. We can rejoice in his grace, free from the compulsion to earn his love and acceptance, and we can live in the peace that comes only through his lordship in our lives. Our God reigns—that is, indeed, "good news."

Application

1. Have I ever felt that life was "out of control"? Why?

2. What does it mean in practical terms to know that "Our God reigns"?

Reviewing This Week

Verses   **Personal Application**

Colossians 3:13

Matthew 6:14-15

Ephesians 4:32

Luke 17:3-4

Mark 11:25

2 Corinthians 5:18-19

Isaiah 52:7

Day 1—Hard Bargain

Memory Verse: Mark 11:24
Therefore I tell you, whatever you ask for in prayer, believe that you have received it, and it will be yours.

"I've been praying," Jennifer declared confidently. "I told God I'd give him a tithe of that five million when I win the sweepstakes."

Her friend Cindi laughed. "Well, then, you don't have a chance. I told him I'd give him half!"

Can we, as Mark 11:24 seems to imply, pray for anything, absolutely anything, and expect that the Lord will come through? Can we pray with assurance for new cars, mink coats, or trips to the Caribbean? The verse seems to be a troublesome one, especially when we try it out and our prayers aren't answered in the way we expected.

But seen in context, Mark 11:24 gives us a much broader picture of the kind of prayer Jesus meant. The verse appears in the framework of Jesus' ministry—cleansing the temple, correcting the Pharisees, commanding forgiveness, discussing his authority. The condition for the fulfillment of Mark 11:24, if Jesus' actions are any indication, is fulfilling the will and purpose of God.

Such a condition for powerful prayer involves much more than attaching an "if it be Thy will" clause onto the end of our prayers. We need to know God's will and walk in it, seeking his kingdom first, and drawing close to him. Then, as our hearts are right with him, what we ask in prayer is likely to be congruent with the mind and purposes of Christ. We are less likely to pray selfishly, and more likely to share God's priorities, as we get to know him. And as we deepen in our knowledge of him, as his will becomes our will, his promise for answered prayer takes on new dimensions.

Application

1. What is the connection between knowing God's will and praying effectively?

2. What changes need to take place in my life so that I might pray with greater power?

Day 2—Due Season

Memory Verse: Galatians 6:9
Let us not become weary in doing good, for at the proper time we will reap a harvest if we do not give up.

Jackie's preschool class took on an exciting project: they were going to grow flowers from seeds. Each child took the seed, planted it carefully in the bedding soil, watered, and waited. But Jackie couldn't wait. Every day for a week he ran to the window box, looked for his plants, poked, prodded, unplanted the seeds and then planted them back again. "It's no use," he pouted after the first week. "Nothin's gonna grow in there."

We live in an instant society—microwave dinners, quick fixes, easy answers. We are conditioned by our environment to expect—even to demand—immediate response, and when we have to wait, we become impatient and irritable.

Paul's exhortation to the Galatians, "Let us not become weary in doing good," is as appropriate for twentieth-century believers as it was for the new church at Galatia. We lose motivation when we don't see results, and weariness sets in. If our work does not seem to be producing as we hope, we want to abandon it and move on to a new project.

But God says, "You *will* reap a harvest if you don't give up." We give up too soon in our prayers for a loved one's salvation. We abandon hope too readily when we don't see spiritual growth in our own lives, when our investment in another's spiritual maturity seems to have no return. The Lord says, "The harvest is coming; be patient; trust me."

In due season the harvest comes; when it's the right time. When the seed has had time to germinate, when the roots are strong enough, when the conditions are right, the reaping time will come. But we must be willing to wait for the *due season*, the moment of ripeness, when our labor brings its return.

Application

1. Have I ever felt that my spiritual labors have produced no harvest at all?

2. What does It mean to my own spiritual growth that there is a "due season" for reaping the harvest?

Day 3—All I Need

Memory Verse: Philippians 4:19
And my God will meet all your needs according to his glorious riches in Christ Jesus.

"But Mom, I really *need* these!" The strident voice of a teenage girl rose above the hum of voices in the department store. The item in question was a pair of eighty-dollar blue Jeans, faded, bleached, and torn in the right knee. Style. Fashion. Self-image. The girl may not have *needed* the jeans to enhance her wardrobe, but she obviously felt that she *needed* them to enhance her acceptability among her peers.

Philippians 4:19 promises that God "will meet all your needs according to his glorious riches in Christ Jesus." But just what needs does this promise cover? My need for a bigger house? A better job? An eighty-dollar pair of Calvin Kleins?

Certainly God knows and cares about the physical, superficial needs of our lives, and he provides what we need to sustain life. But God's priority goes much deeper than the kind of radial tires we buy or the brand name on our back pockets. God is interested in eternal values, in spiritual needs, and he knows what we need in our lives to draw us closer to him. "Out of his glorious riches in Christ Jesus," God will enrich us spiritually.

The application of Philippians 4:19 involves *trusting* God to know and care about our *real* needs, the deep needs of our souls, and allowing him the freedom to order our circumstances so that those needs are met. When we are bold enough to pray, "Lord, do whatever is necessary to make me like Jesus Christ," our Father delights to answer that prayer and supply our needs.

Application

1. What is the difference between my "needs" and my "wants"?

2. What spiritual needs can I identify in my life?

3. How can this verse help me keep my own priorities in line with God's value system?

Day 4—Giving and Receiving

Memory Verse: Luke 6:38

Give, and it will be given to you. A good measure, pressed down, shaken together and running over, will be poured into your lap. For with the measure you use, it will be measured to you.

"Just give to the Lord," the voice on the radio declared. "Give, and he will give back to you, a hundredfold." The preacher went on to explain how an old woman on social security had sent her last ten dollars to support his ministry, and the next day she got an anonymous money order for a thousand dollars. "The Lord will be faithful to his Word," the preacher concluded. "You give, and you'll receive."

The Lord is, of course, faithful to his Word. But many well-meaning Christians have interpreted Luke 6:38 as a "payment in kind" bargain with God: if I give God my dollar, he's obliged to return it to me with interest. This "seed-sowing" fallacy, where twenty dollars supposedly becomes two thousand dollars by an act of divine multiplication, has caused much disappointment and frustration.

The "giving and receiving" principle is a valid one; the Lord does, indeed, say, "Give, and it will be given to you," but he does not specify exactly what the "return" will be. The verse appears in the context of forgiveness, of not judging; the principle is not *investment*, in any material sense, but *generosity*.

As we give, as we forgive, as we are compassionate with others, we take on the character of the Lord himself. He is generous and giving, and he gives to us as we give ourselves in love to others.

Application

1. Have I ever "given" to God or to others as a bribe, to get something in return?

2. What is God's concept of giving, as demonstrated in the gift of Jesus Christ?

3. How can this verse help me learn to give more selflessly?

Day 5—The Way Out

Memory Verse: 1 Corinthians 10:13
No temptation has seized you except what is common to man. And God is faithful; he will not let you be tempted beyond what you can bear. But when you are tempted, he will also provide a way out so that you can stand up under it.

Becky had experienced some hard knocks in the past few weeks; the stress was beginning to show, and she wasn't sure she could handle anything else. "Why me?" Becky wept, covering her face. "I just can't stand any more! I can't pay my bills; I just lost my job, and now my car broke down on the highway. How much more of this can I take?"

Some people seem to have more than their share of trouble and temptation. Within six months, one family faced financial trouble, cancer, quadruple bypass surgery, and leukemia; their trials brought them face to face with anger, bitterness, and despair as well. Other people seem to go through life with relatively minor stresses and few real temptations to sin.

But whether our problems are great or small, they are part of the common thread that ties humanity together. All of us face temptation; it is, Paul says, "common to man." But Paul assures us that "God . . . will not let you be tempted beyond what you can bear."

Often what we can bear is more than what we *think* we can bear. God will use the troubled times in our lives for our maturity in him, but he promises as well that he will not let temptation break us. He will provide "a way out," "a way of escape."

Sometimes the "way out" is true escape, being removed from what caused the trouble. At other times, rather than being removed from it, we must withstand the stress, face the temptation, endure the pain. Whether we escape or endure, God is faithful to provide what we need; we can trust him not to give us more than we can bear.

Application

1. Have I ever faced more stress or temptation than I thought I could bear?

2. Under what circumstances has God provided an "escape" for me? When have I had to walk "through" my difficulties?

3. How can today's verse encourage me when times are tough?

Day 6—Humility and Exaltation

Memory Verses: 1 Peter 5:6-7
Humble yourselves, therefore, under God's mighty hand, that he may lift you up in due time. Cast all your anxiety on him because he cares for you.

"I was so humble I was given an award for humility," the pastor quipped. "They gave me a humility plaque—but they had to take it back when I hung it on my office wall."

Humility is rare among twentieth-century Christians. Our pride takes two seemingly contradictory forms: self-exaltation and self-denial. But both focus on *self,* not on God.

Francois Fenelon, seventeenth-century French archbishop, wrote:

> He who so completely forgets himself that he never thinks of self . . . is truly humble. If we had the light to discern it, we should see clearly that when we think we are humbling ourselves we are exalting ourselves; when we think we are annihilating ourselves we are seeking our own life.[3]

True humility, as Fenelon implies, means recognizing who we are in light of who God is. Excess of self-importance and low self-worth are *both* self-centered perspectives; true humility is God-centered.

When we humble ourselves, we become intensely aware of God and less aware of ourselves. We can focus on his face and get our eyes off our own image. We can stop worrying about how others perceive us. Such humbling is difficult—as one seventy-year-old saint joked, "It ain't the heat that gets you, it's the humility." But when we submit to him and feel the weight of the "mighty hand of God" upon us, we can forget ourselves, abandon ourselves to his presence, and cast our cares upon him.

Application

1. What form does my pride usually take—self-exaltation or self-degradation?

2. Why must I humble myself in order for the Lord to lift me up?

[3]Francois Fenelon, "Letters of Spiritual Counsel," in *Spiritual Disciplines*, ed. Sherwood Wirt (Westchester, IL: Crossway Books, 1983), 69-71.

Day 7—Support System

Memory Verse: Deuteronomy 33:27
The eternal God is your refuge, and underneath are the everlasting arms. He will drive out your enemy before you, saying, "Destroy him!"

Misty was only four when her parents divorced. Her dad moved away, and the following summer she went with her grandparents to visit him in his new apartment. In the swimming pool one afternoon, Grandpa stood Misty on the side of the pool, held out his arms, and called, "Jump!"

But Misty, normally a little fish, suddenly seemed afraid of the water, and stood trembling on the sidewalk shaking her head.

"Jump, Misty—I'll catch you!"

"Are you sure, Grandpa?"

"Of course I'm sure! Jump!"

But Misty wouldn't jump. Finally Grandpa, a bit irritated, said, "Misty, do you think I won't catch you? Do you think I'll just walk away?"

The tears spilled over, and Misty sobbed. "Daddy did!"

Human support systems often fail us. We disappoint those we love, and are disappointed by them. People simply aren't there for us when we need them most.

But God promises that with him things are different. He's always there, always listening, always caring, always ready to support us. "Underneath are the everlasting arms."

Sometimes those arms reach out clothed in flesh, in the warm embrace of a loved one. Sometimes they support us through the Word, sometimes through the quiet peace that comes in prayer. Sometimes we are not aware of them at all, but they still hold us up, supporting, surrounding, loving. Underneath us are the everlasting arms.

Application

1. Have I ever felt abandoned by someone I loved and depended upon?

2. How have I experienced the faithfulness of God's "everlasting arms"?

3. How can this verse help me in times when I feel my supports have given way?

Reviewing This Week

Verses   **Personal Application**

Mark 11:24

Galatians 6:9

Philippians 4:19

Luke 6:38

1 Corinthians 10:13

1 Peter 5:6-7

Deuteronomy 33:27

Day 1—A Circle of Light

Memory Verse: John 8:12

When Jesus spoke again to the people, he said, "I am the light of the world. Whoever follows me will never walk in darkness, but will have the light of life."

When Judy Garland stepped onstage, she filled the spotlight. Nothing was illuminated but her face, and as she sang, her listeners had a sense of being transported beyond themselves into the meaning of her song. The focus of reality, at that moment, was "Judy," and everything else faded into the dim recesses of the shadowed room. The spotlight brought her into sharp focus as the center of attention, and all around her was darkness.

When the Scripture speaks of Jesus as "the light," the image is not of thousands of blazing bulbs lighting up a football field for a night game. Rather, he is like a hand-held lamp that throws a circle of light in the immediate vicinity. Such a lamp lights the path that a traveler will walk, but lights it only one step at a time.

Jesus is the center of that circle of light. As we follow him, we share the light, but he is always at center. Jesus Christ is the focal point, and everything else fades into dim gray by comparison.

If we are to keep our lives illuminated, to have his light falling upon the road we walk, we must stay close to him. Jesus does not hand the lamp to us and suggest that we go the way he wants; he, the Light, leads, and if we want to stay in the light, we follow.

Application

1. Have I ever tried to go my own way, apart from the Light? What was the result?

2. How can this verse help me remember the importance of staying close to Jesus?

Day 2—God's Purpose: The Image of Christ

Memory Verses: Romans 8:28-29

And we know that in all things God works for the good of those who love him, who have been called according to his purpose. For those God foreknew he also predestined to be conformed to the likeness of his Son, that he might be firstborn among many brothers.

A baby dies of Sudden Infant Death Syndrome, and the parents are devastated, plagued with guilt, and asking, "Why?" A seventeen-year-old plunges headfirst into a pond and rises to the surface a quadriplegic. A single mother of three, struck down by leukemia, has to release her children to foster homes.

And in all these cases, well-meaning Christians stand by and attempt to comfort: "All things work together for good, you know," they say blithely. "Just trust God, and praise him for everything."

Such pat answers are often repeated because they *do* contain an element of truth; they become "pat," meaningless, and superficial, when they are used as a panacea for all ills, whether the cure fits or not.

The truth is, God does use everything for the benefit of his people—even disaster and tragedy. Romans 8:28 says, "In all things God works. . . ." God does not cause human suffering. He is not the author of pain and misery. But what the Enemy of our souls intends for destruction, God can use for growth.

The key to understanding Romans 8:28 is Romans 8:29. The Lord makes clear what "his purpose" is: that we be "conformed to the likeness of his Son." Everything that happens is not good, but nothing is wasted in the economy of God. Even the sorrow, misfortune, and calamity that strike all of us can be used by the Spirit to transform us into the image of Christ.

Application

1. Have I ever had experiences that made me doubt that "all things work together for good"?

2. How does Romans 8:29 clarify Romans 8:28?

3. How can these verses help me deal with the struggles I have in my own life?

Day 3—The Promise of Completion

Memory Verse: Philippians 1:6
Being confident of this, that he who began a good work in you will carry it on to completion until the day of Christ Jesus.

"Elizabeth is a good student," the note on the side of the report card read, "but she doesn't finish what she starts. She has a lot of good ideas, but rarely brings them to completion."

Many of us are like Elizabeth. We start into a new venture with high hopes and great motivation. But somewhere along the way, we become discouraged. Someone tells us that our ideas are stupid, or that we are not capable of doing what we dream. We get to a particularly difficult hurdle and give up.

Sometimes we feel the Christian life is like that, too. We start well, and believe that in Christ we can accomplish anything. But then our prayers become rote, our Bible reading ritual. We can't seem to regain that sense of God's presence; we have, we conclude, "lost our first love."

But God has a different perspective. He began the work of salvation in us; he leads and guides us in his will, and he will complete what he has begun. Often we fail to see God's grace in the ongoing process of walking with him because his agenda is different from ours. We know what we *want* to see happen in our lives; God knows what *needs* to happen.

"When I first came into a relationship with Christ," one woman explained, "I knew I had a lot of changing to do. But, strangely enough, the things God changed weren't on my list at all!"

When God begins his work in our lives, he has a plan for our maturity. He is Alpha and Omega, the Beginning and the End. And what God has begun, he will finish.

Application

1. Have I ever tried to "decide" for God what problems in my life needed dealing with?

2. Has God ever pointed out issues that were a surprise to me?

3. How can today's verse help me relax in God's will and have confidence in the direction of my life?

Day 4—Send for Help!

Memory Verse: James 1:5
If any of you lacks wisdom, he should ask God, who gives generously to all without finding fault, and it will be given to him.

A new employee in an electronics plant had the responsibility for overseeing one machine. The machine worked fine when the young man came on duty, but soon it began to run a bit rough. The employee tinkered with the machine, trying to "fix" it, until finally it stopped working altogether.

In fear and trembling the worker sent for the foreman, and stammered, "I—I, well, sir, I did my best to fix it."

"Son," the foreman thundered, "you need to know only one thing. Around here, doing your best means sending for me!"

Wisdom, James 1:5 says, has its source in God alone. And if we are to attain wisdom, we need to learn that doing our best means sending for God.

Often we spend time tinkering with our lives or the lives of others. We don't think to ask God for his wisdom in the decisions we must make; instead, we use our human reasoning and take our best guess.

But the path to wisdom does not lie in guesswork. The Scriptures give us clear indication of God's direction for his people, and through Bible study, application, prayer, and meditation, we can understand what God wants to reveal to us.

"If any of you lacks wisdom," James says, "he should ask God, who gives generously to all without finding fault, and it will be given to him." The first step to attaining wisdom is recognizing that we are not wise. The second step is to ask. And God, who is faithful to his Word and His people, will respond.

Application

1. Under what circumstances have I tinkered with my life, making it worse rather than fixing it?

2. What practical steps can I take to ask God for wisdom?

Day 5—Waiting for the Wind

Memory Verse: Isaiah 40:31
But those who hope in the Lord will renew their strength. They will soar on wings like eagles; they will run and not grow weary, they will walk and not be faint.

High above civilization, alone on his craggy peak, the eagle waits. He watches, senses, and then, with an effortless grace, he spreads his wings and soars. He does not flap frantically to gain altitude, he merely turns his wings into the wind and rises.

Isaiah 40:31 promises that we, too, can be like the eagle, mounting up on wings, soaring effortlessly, without weariness. But this is not often our experience. We usually flap around like invalid pigeons, scratching for mere existence, flying only when our place in the park is disturbed.

We need to learn to wait on the Lord. Like the wind that raises the eagle to his heights, the wind of the Spirit will lift us up as well—beyond the weariness of daily life, beyond the struggle for existence, beyond the plodding pace of normal interaction.

But the eagle does not rise without plunging from the cliff into the wind. His ability to stay aloft is based on his understanding of wind currents; when the wind is against him, he rises. He waits on the cliff until the right moment, then allows the contrary breezes to lift him up.

Most of us are grounded by winds that are against us. We give up and never take the first flight. We fear the plunge from the cliff into the buoyant breath of God, and so we stand fixed, afraid to launch out.

But when we do take the risk, when we wait upon the Lord, and then give ourselves in obedience to a free-fall from the cliffs of his will, we discover that there is rest in soaring with him. We do not have to struggle; we have only to fly, and in flying, to find new strength.

Application

1. Why is "waiting upon the Lord" essential to "mounting up with wings as the eagle"?

2. How can this verse help me be more willing to take risks in God's will?

Day 6—Through the Fire

Memory Verse: Isaiah 43:2
When you pass through the waters, I will be with you; and when you pass through the rivers, they will not sweep over you. When you walk through the fire, you will not be burned; the flames will not set you ablaze.

In the Book of Daniel, three young men provide one of the world's best-known Bible stories. Shadrach, Meshach, and Abednego, three of the finest young men of Israel, were taken into captivity to Babylon. There King Nebuchadnezzar, filled with his own importance, commanded that everyone bow down and worship his image.

When Shadrach, Meshach, and Abednego refused to worship anyone except the One True God, they were cast into Nebuchadnezzar's furnace of fire.

Isaiah 43:2 brings their experience into focus for us. There the Lord says, "When you pass through the fire . . . when you walk through the water . . ." Not if, but *when*. If we are committed to serving and honoring the Lord, at some point we will be faced with "passing through the fire" for him. We may not face a physical furnace, but we may face the fires of persecution, anger, hostility, or suffering. And God says: "I will be with you."

When the three young Israelites stepped into the king's furnace, all the people looked and saw, not three, but *four* men in the fire, their bonds burned away, walking freely among the flames. They did not escape the fate decreed for them. But the Lord was with them in the fire, as surely as he has promised to be with us in the flood and fire that life brings to us. The promise of God remains: "I will be with you; the waters will not overflow, nor will the flames burn you."

Application

1. What kinds of "fires" and "floods" have I experienced?

2. How was I aware of the Lord's presence with me?

Day 7—Upheld by His Hand

Memory Verse: Isaiah 41:10
So do not fear, for I am with you; do not be dismayed, for I am your God. I will strengthen you and help you; I will uphold you with my righteous right hand.

Beth had the same recurring nightmare: she was running along a cliff, then she slipped, and fell headlong, into a bottomless ravine. Falling, without control, without end, falling, falling, falling. . . .

Beth's dream may be one many of us identify with. The sense of losing control can be nightmarish, and we may fear falling without end, without remedy. Financial failure may be the chasm that we face, or professional disgrace. Personal relationships may go out of control, and we look into a never-ending ravine of pain and misunderstanding.

But God says, "Don't be afraid; I am holding you up." Like the father who helps his child learn to swim, God holds us above the water. We may not feel his hands; indeed, we may suspect that he lets us go just so we can do it on our own. But he promises that he doesn't let go. "I am with you," he declares. "I give you strength and hold you up."

God's promise never to let go takes on new meaning in a world where relationships are temporary and life is uncertain. We do not need to fear, for he is with us. We can relax and stop striving, for he is our God. His strength becomes ours; amid all our sin and rebellion, he undergirds us with his righteousness. We cannot fall, for he holds us firm.

Application

1. Under what circumstances have I felt myself "falling"?

2. How does God's promise in Isaiah 41:10 help me to have faith in the midst of my fears?

Reviewing This Week

Verses   **Personal Application**

John 8:12

Romans 8:28-29

Philippians 1:6

James 1:5

Isaiah 40:31

Isaiah 43:2

Isaiah 41:10